MAKING STUFF FOR KIDS

black dog
publishing

CONTENTS

INTRODUCTION

VICTORIA WOODCOCK

CHILDREN OF THE REVOLUTION

In the precursor to this book, 2006's *Making Stuff: An Alternative Craft Book*, my introduction charted the rise of crafting as a hip pastime. By now I'm sure you know the score: grannified knitting circles had morphed into cocktail-quaffing stitch 'n' bitch groups, online craft communities such as Craftster were thriving, and alternative craft fairs, selling things that twentysomethings actually wanted to buy, abounded. It wasn't that the way of crafting itself had changed, but that the quirky, indie-side of craft had become increasing visible as a collective movement.

The so-called craft revolution has been commented on far and wide, and fortunately the increased interest in craft and DIY shows no sign of abating, as the media frenzy that it stirred up has done. Craft communities continue to form and flourish and craftsters are becoming increasingly powerful on a global scale. For example, regional branches of the Craft Mafia group that first started in Austin, Texas have found their way across the Atlantic to Leeds, Glasgow and Manchester; and the online craft selling and buying portal, Etsy, has recorded sales well into the millions with registered users spanning 60 countries.

But enough of the adults! Whereas grown-ups often seem slightly bemused by the idea of crafting, kids and crafts go together like, well, paper and pens, or needle and thread. "Kids are natural makers," explains *Making Stuff For Kids* contributor Susan Rowe Harrison, and crafty parents such as fellow contributors Aoife Clifford and Heidi Kenney all seem to agree that kids and crafting go hand in hand. "I always did some crafting and making things, such as knitting, but there was definitely a craft explosion once I had kids," says Aoife. Heidi remembers that she "got into making stuff with a fury" after the birth of her youngest son. "I am not sure why this might be the case," expands Heidi. "Maybe it's something to do with connecting fond childhood 'making' memories with your own children, or wanting to create things for them."

Nearly everyone I spoke to about this book started to energetically recount fond memories of their childhood craft activities: potato printing, cereal box theatres, papier-mâché, etc., many of which appear in this book. The desire to share these memories is well-explained by Claire Armitstead writing in *The Guardian* about taking her daughter to a pottery class: "One of the best things about being a parent is a chance to explore memories of your own childhood while experiencing them afresh through the enjoyment of your child."

At the same time, crafting with kids can also be a conscious decision to actively encourage creativity. Craft enthusiasts all seem to agree that making stuff adds balance to a child's leisure time and teaches them important skills such as using imagination, dexterity and problem-solving. For Aoife Clifford, craft is a great way of teaching children patience, "but that is secondary to the fun you have while doing it."

In fact, in our technological era, crafting seems to be the perfect antidote to the overuse of—or even addiction to—computer games, television and the Internet. One idea behind the resurgence of craft is that as our lives become increasingly involved with technology, the more we crave pastimes that are based in physical reality. "I think [crafting] is a reaction to most people's work these days—paperwork that just gets filed somewhere, being a small part of a much bigger whole," says Aoife Clifford. "To make something from the beginning yourself, especially if it was your own idea, is really rewarding."

My very own crafty mum limited television watching (much to my classmates' horror, I wasn't allowed to watch the popular Australian soap, *Neighbours*!) in favour of potato printing and playdough-making. And if this isn't example enough of the benefits of crafting for a young mind, the editor of online kids crafting mecca Kiddley (see the Directory on page 156 for details), Claire Robertson, sets out her ethos thus: "We live in a house where the TV buzzes on from time to time, and computer games aren't blacklisted, but we also try to fill most of our days with mess and craft and mud and drifts of flour." It's a bit on the yummy mummy side, but certainly appealing!

And then there's the social aspect that has inspired craft groups throughout the ages: you can make stuff and natter at the same time. "I love to do any kind of craft activity with my daughter as we get to spend time together chatting and creating," says all-round craft maven and contributor, Michelle Duxbury-Townsley, and Cindy Hopper, another crafty mum, surely hits the nail on the head when she says "doing crafts with children is a wonderful way to bond with them".

But can today's hip kids and savvy tweens, armed with an increasing array of virtual pastimes, really be talked into a spot of tie-dying or knitting? As the craft resurgence of recent years has shown, injecting age-old methods like knitting with a drop of rock and roll, should do the trick. So, whilst corn-dollies may not be on the agenda, a button necklace, or ballsy cross-stitch may well hit the spot. Crafts have moved with the times and techno-kids can use modern methods such as taking digital photos for the project on page xxx, or printing off images from the Internet to use as stencils.

Heidi Kenney, who runs My Paper Crane, a website full of weird and wonderful soft toy creations, suggests encouraging "gross projects, like homemade slime" and reckons that even sewing can be made more appealing by upping the gross factor. "My son once created and sewed his own snot doll," she says. "I think it's a fun way to get the kids excited about making stuff; when it is cool and slightly taboo."

But every budding crafter will be different, and whilst snot dolls may appeal to one, stylish makes will lure in another. A quick flick through the September 2007 edition of *Teen Vogue* will tell you that crafting is anything but dorky. In the A–Z Fall Fashion Guide, nestled between "C is for Crowns" (as seen on the Marc by Marc Jacobs runway of course) and "E is for Eco-chic" is—you guessed it—"D is for Do-it-yourself".

Designer *du jour*, Philip Lim, shares some customising tips, whilst a handcrafted tie-dye top is given high-fashion status.

In the pages of *Vogue*, appearance may be everything, but when crafting with kids it is very much the taking part that counts. "Don't worry about the mess, and don't worry if you end up making something completely different from what you intended," advises Aoife. Cindy Hopper reminds us that it is important to "focus more on the process than the final product. It is in the process that the fun and learning takes place." Michelle Duxbury-Townsley's top-tip is: "Just go for it! It's not about being perfect."

And finally, a word of warning: if you are craftily inclined and don't have kids (like myself—I'm far too young of course!), this book might make you want to have them! Or at least borrow some for the day... But equally, many of these projects can be enjoyed by adults: I rediscovered the pleasures of papier-mâché whilst putting together this book, and older crafters could learn a thing or two from their younger counterparts. The popular craft night, Hungamunga, held at the Bethnal Green Working Men's club (no longer actually a working men's club; more of a hipster hangout) in London, is essentially a load of grown-ups rediscovering the simple pleasures of making a bit of mess with anything you have to hand. And with that, I'll leave it to Aoife Clifford to sum up: "Sometimes [the craft world] treats itself a bit too seriously, making it 'cool' can lose a bit of the original essence and inspiration—so maybe the craft movement should take off its sunglasses, put down its vodka tonic and get inspired by the originality of kids crafting."

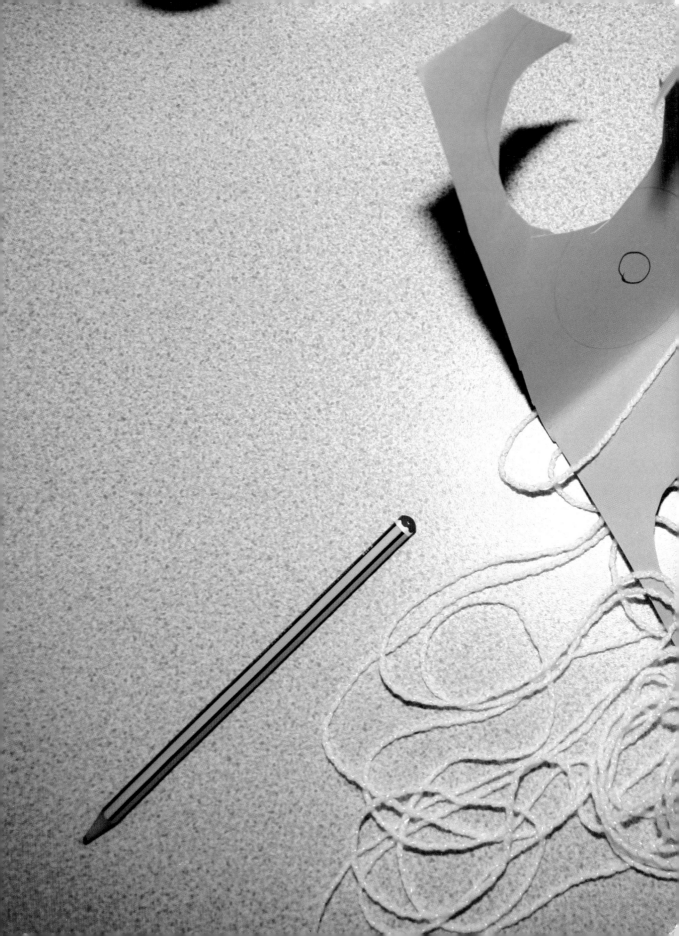

GETTING STARTED

Now, you're keen to get started, right? But before you begin, here is how to use this book to best effect.

TEENY TALENTS, CUNNING CRAFTERS, SUPER SKILLS OR TOUGH COOKIES?

The book is divided into four sections: Teeny Talents, Cunning Crafters, Super Skills and Tough Cookies. On the Contents page you will see that each sections corresponds to an age range. This is a rough guide only, as levels of concentration and dexterity vary dramatically between individuals. So, certain six year-olds might have already progressed from Teeny Talents to Cunning Crafters!

Feel free to flick through all the projects—you might find something you simply have to make! In that case you can always enlist the help of older or younger brothers, sisters or friends, and of course, adults.

THE KEY TO SUCCESS

Look out for these symbols throughout the book, as they will help you decide whether the project is suitable for you.

| Adult supervision needed (more than usual) | Mess will be made! | Takes time (and patience!) |

A is for adults

This book is designed for adults and children to read and use together. Adults are great at doing all the boring and dangerous bits—like sawing wood, or machine sewing seams. This will leave you to do all the fun decorating stages!

 It is very important that you and an adult read through all stages of a project first and look out this symbol.

This lets you know that the project has one or more stages that must be carried out by, or be heavily supervised by, an adult. These stages might involve sharp objects, like craft knives or scissors, something hot like boiling water or an iron, or strong chemicals, like some glues or bleach (which is used for the Bleach Party on page 113).

The Tough Cookie section is for adults only, but there are still some stages in these projects that you can help out with, such as painting the wood panels of the Cheesy Toy Box (see page 148).

Messy pup

This symbol shows that this project is likely to be quite messy—so remember to get yourself and your work surface well covered!

All the time in the world

 This symbol means that this project may take quite a while to get finished, or can't be done all in one go. So, if you only have one crafternoon, this project may not be suitable. Allow yourself plenty of time to plan and carry out this project—possibly a couple of days.

•••

In order to get crafty you will need some supplies—so make sure an adult has a look at the basic kit below—this is all great stuff to have ready in the house and will come in useful for almost everything in the book. So, without further ado, happy crafting!

•••

Keep a stash of paints, paper, glue, and an assortment of bits and bobs to hand—in preparation for the oncoming craft attack!

Paper

For painting and colouring, paper a bit thicker than normal A4 (8.3×11.7 inch) printer paper is required. Look out for pads of drawing paper and coloured sugar paper. Also keep scrap paper. Colourful bits of paper can be found all over the place: save envelopes from birthday cards, samples of wallpaper, etc..

Newspaper

A stash of newspapers should always be to hand. Not only can you make amazing papier-mâché creations with it, it should be used to cover tabletops whenever the paints come out to play.

Cardboard

Reuse and recycle! Shoeboxes, cereal boxes and toilet rolls are works of art waiting to happen. If you need a big sheet of nice coloured card, an art supply shop is the only answer. Old birthday and Christmas cards can be cut up to make new ones—just add glitter.

Paints

Poster paints are the best bet for budding artists as they are washable and non-toxic. They usually come in squirty bottles. Never, ever, use oil based paints with kids. Get basic prime colours (red, yellow and blue), black and white to start with. You can add white to lighten the shade and black to darken it.
Try mixing colours:

red + yellow = orange
blue + yellow = green
red + **blue** = purple (but sometimes brown!)

There is only so much you can achieve by mixing paint; if you want a shocking pink or a lime green you will need to go out and buy a tube in this colour.

Paintbrushes

Get a cheap kit with a variety of shapes and sizes — don't buy artists' quality, as they will only get messed up. Foam brushes can also be widely found and are great for young kids.

Spatulas

You can buy plastic spatulas—along with paintbrushes they are useful for spreading glue. You can make a spatula by cutting up a plastic container and sanding the edges. Lollypop sticks are good at dabbing glue on one small spot.

Paint Pots

Used yoghurt pots are perfect for holding paint and PVA glue. To make a cunning mess-free paint pot, use a plastic container with a clip on lid. Cut a small hole in the middle of the lid—this is where the paintbrush goes.

Glue

The most versatile of glues is PVA. Glue sticks are handy and non-messy for small projects, but they don't have a lot of sticking power. Fabric glue is, well, for fabric. A good glue to have stashed away is non-toxic, multipurpose strong glue that comes in a metal tube. Some of the projects use Epoxy Resin for hardcore gluing projects and it should only be used by adults. Some projects use a hot glue gun, which should only be used by adults or older children under supervision.

Don't use super glue, even if you are a grown-up—it really does glue your fingers together! And then it brings the skin off—nasty.

Fabric scraps
Fabric is not just for sewing. Old clothes can be cut up and used to make new stuff, like clothes for peg dolls, but also stuck to paper and card to make pictures and patterns.

Scissors
To cut paper, safety scissors will do the trick. For cutting fabric and card though you will need a pair of much sharper scissors.

Craft knifes
Craft knifes can be easily found art supply stores. They generally come with a metal pen-like stem and an interchangeable blade at the end. They are useful for cutting out shapes from paper and card neatly and precisely. This means that craft knives are super-sharp: they are not for young children and older children need adult supervision. Oh, and they should be stored somewhere out of the reach of children. You need to use a cutting mat with your knife, to avoid cutting into the table, and using them with a metal ruler will create perfect straight lines.

Hammers, drills and saws
Your best bet on this front is to make friends with someone who has a fully equipped workshop and get him or her to operate the tools for you—you can be the creative director of their manual labour! But seriously, tools such as saws and drills are dangerous. It's always a good idea to wear goggles when using any wood tools —they are really cheap from DIY stores and protect your eyes from dust and debris whilst looking cool!

Smock it to 'em!
Things can get a little bit messy with many of the projects in this book. Check out the awesome smocks worn by Aoife Clifford's crafty kids on page 62. They were handmade a few generations ago and worn by her husband and his brother as children. Keep yourself clean in a DIY smock:

1 Wear a large OLD shirt back to front.

2 Make the apron on page 138.
But, don't wear baggy smocks when using electrical tools—they might get caught up.

Stitching, knitting and other stuff
Knitting and sewing require quite specific materials —these are outlined in the How To sections (coming up next). Some projects require specific items that you will have to buy especially. Read through and tick off the materials to make sure you have everything you need before you start.

HOW TO...

CROSS-STITCH

AMY ADAMS

A cross-stitch is simply an X-shaped embroidery stitch worked on a specially designed fabric, called Aida. This fabric is woven in such a way that it has holes that you stitch through, and comes in various different sizes which relate to the number of stitches that can be completed per inch of fabric. For example, a 14-count Aida will require 14 stitches per inch, an 11-count will require 11 stitches per inch, and so on. Cross-stitch is usually completed using stranded cotton embroidery thread. This is made of six threads loosely twisted together. Sometimes you will need to separate these strands into sets of two before you start to stitch (this is the case for the Skull And Cross-Stitch Bones on page 110). You can also get extra large cross-stitch fabric that is 6-count (sometimes called Binca). This is great for beginners and the holes are big enough that you won't need to divide the strands of embroidery thread (see page 100 for a project using Binca). To practice, cut a piece of fabric 20×20 cm and a 40 cm length of embroidery thread. Grab a needle and an embroidery hoop will be helpful too: they come in different sizes, Julie Jackson suggests using a 13 or 15 cm one.

Step one
To place the fabric in the hoop, separate the two loops (by loosening the screw) and lay the Aida across the non-adjustable hoop. Now place the adjustable hoop over the top and press down. Pull the fabric taut like a drum and when it is pulled evenly, tighten the screw. This will help you to see the holes clearly and maintain an even tension.

Step two
Remember to divide the thread unless you are using 6-count Aida/Binca. Thread the needle and pull about 10 cm of thread through the eye. Tie a couple of knots at the other end.

Step three
Hold the hoop in your left hand (unless you are left-handed, in which case use your right hand) and the needle in your other hand. In the middle of the hoop, bring the needle from the back to the front, through one of the holes.

Pull the thread until the knot touches the fabric. Then bring the needle through the hole diagonally opposite —below and to the right. You have now completed the bottom half of your first cross-stitch.

Step four
To complete the top half and create a full cross-stitch, bring the needle back to the front through the hole directly above the one you last went through and then back down again through the hole diagonally opposite but this time to the left. This forms another half cross-stitch in the opposite direction to the one underneath. The second half cross-stitch crosses over the first so that an X is formed. You have now completed your first cross-stitch!

Step five
To stitch a second X, begin the process again, placing the next stitch adjacent to the first.

Tips
When following a cross-stitch pattern, the type of stitch and colour to be used are indicated on the chart. Each square on the chart represents one X stitch.

Keep the tension of your stitches even and light. This will prevent thread from breaking and fabric from puckering.

You can work a large area of cross-stitches by working a horizontal row of half cross-stitches and completing the other half of each X by making an equal number of half-stitches in the reverse direction.

Work in the direction that is comfortable for you, for example, left to right, but be consistent. Remember to always make the first stitch of the X in the same direction, either ╱ or ╲.

KNITTING

CLAIRE MONTGOMERIE AND VICTORIA WOODCOCK

● ●

KNIT KIDS

Hands up, who was taught to knit by their gran? Undoubtedly, the majority of knitters were taught to do so by a member of an older generation, and if you have basic knit knowledge you too can pass on the ancient skill to the new wave of knit wits. Here's how to captivate youngsters with two sticks and string, even if they have got a Wii...

GET TO KNIT!

The simplicity and adaptability of knitting will occupy a young mind for several hours, so long as you can channel the activity. The earliest age to start knitting is somewhere between four and seven years, depending on the motor skills, hand eye coordination, dexterity and concentration span of the individual. By age seven most children can grasp the technique.

The methods used to teach knitting to children are similar to those employed in teaching adults, but there is one important difference: whilst most adults are able to concentrate for long periods and can knit swatches as a learning tool, children want to make fully realised objects, otherwise they quickly lose interest.

Captivate your pupil's imagination from the start by gathering together an array of brightly coloured yarn. Then arm yourself with fun techniques such as finger knitting (explained on page 72), and exciting gadgets like pompom makers (make your own on page 28) and French knitting (see page 84) to vary the tricky task of learning to knit.

● ●

THE KNIT KIT

● ●

Sticks

Knitting needles are made in a variety of materials—metal, plastic, bamboo and wood are the most common ones. Bamboo or plastic needles are best for kids as they are more pliable, making them easier and more comfortable to knit with. Shy away from metal needles as they are cold, slippery, and hard to get to grips with —not to mention dangerous if the young knitter wants to have a sword fight!

Needles also come in different lengths and thicknesses. The longer the needles the more stitches you can fit on, but shorter ones are easier for little hands to handle. In the UK the width is measured in mm (and by a different point system in the US) and is referred to as the needle size. The size you use depends on the thickness of your yarn.

The bigger the needles, the bigger the stitches, and the quicker your knitting will grow! However, don't be tempted to use very large needles; it is much harder to get the technique right when knitting with chunky needles. Opt for a 4 mm to 6 mm needle, with yarn to match (see the String section below).

String

Basically you can knit with any long string, the most common being balls of yarn. The label will tell you everything you need to know about your yarn: what the fibre is (wool, cotton, acrylic, etc.) and importantly, what size needles to use. It's pretty simple really, the thicker the yarn the thicker the needles you will need. Ask the shop assistant to help you match yarn and needles.

When learning to knit opt for wool or acrylic (or a mix of the two) as they are soft and have a slight stretch. Stay away from rigid fibres like cotton as they take some getting used to. Children are often very tight knitters at first, so the springy nature of wool or acrylic will help them move the needles through the loops. If your learner knits very tightly, try using needles that are a few sizes too big for the yarn.

It is better to use a smooth yarn without bobbles—this will make it easier to see the individual stitches and to insert the needle. Fancy yarns should be reserved for pompom making!

Things

For the projects in this book all you will need other than sticks and string is scissors, maybe a few dressmaker's pins, and a yarn needle (a big chunky knitting needle with a blunt tip—you can get plastic ones that are great for kids). Oh, and a medium-sized crochet hook for fixing mistakes!

• •

GETTING STARTED

There are a couple of things to do before you can hand over the sticks to a rookie knitter. The first is to make a slip-knot.

• •

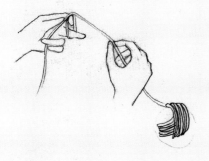  

1 Take a length of yarn about 30 cm along and make a small loop, crossing over the yarn from the tail and the yarn that connects to the ball. Hold the point where they cross between your fingers.

2 With your spare hand, stick a finger through the loop, hook the yarn attached to the ball and bring it through the circle, forming a new loop. Keep hold of this loop and let go of the original circle.

3 Pull the tail end tight to form a knot at the bottom of the loop. Push a needle through the loop and pull both yarns so that the knot slips to the size of the needle.

DOUBLE CAST ON (AKA LONG TAIL CAST ON)

The most helpful tip when teaching anybody to knit is to cast on for him or her. Cast on a nice, even number of stitches—20 works well, as it is easy to remember and not too many to count for a child.

1 Hold the needle with the slip-knot on it in your right hand. Hold the two yarns apart by wrapping the tail end of the yarn around your left thumb and the yarn attached to the ball over your index finger. Keep the remainder of the yarn out of the way by covering it in your palm with your remaining left hand fingers.

2 Place the tip of the needle under the yarn that runs from palm to thumb and pick it up.

3 Make sure this yarn stays on the needle (pop a finger on top of it if you need to) then dip the needle under the yarn that runs from the index finger to the needle, moving the needle towards your thumb and bring it through the space you will see between the two yarns to the thumb.

4 Move your thumb out of the loop and pull on the tail to tighten the stitch (don't pull so tight that the yarn is stretched, or your first row of knitting will be really awkward). Repeat until you have as many stitches as you need.

THIS IS KNIT

The first few rows are the most fiddly as they can be quite tight, so knit a couple before you hand over the reins. Guide your pupil's hands through the actions at first. After just a few stitches back off and talk them through the motions instead. Here's a handy rhyme to help remember the knit stitch:

In through the front door

1 Hold the needle with the cast on stitches on it in your left hand and the empty needle in your right. The yarn also goes in your right hand (try weaving it between your fingers to keep hold of it) behind the needles. Stick the tip of the right hand needle into the first loop, from left to right.

Around to the back

2 Bring the yarn over the point of the right hand needle in a clockwise motion, using your index finger. To steady the motion, grip the two needles between the thumb and index finger on your left hand whilst your right hand wraps the yarn.

Poke your head through the window

3 Take control of the right needle again and bring it back out of the loop you pushed it into. Easy enough, except you need to pull the yarn that is over the tip back through the loop with it. You now have a loop on the right hand needle.

Off jumps Jack

4 Push the right hand needle a little further through the loop and move it over to the right so that the original loop slides off the tip of the left needle. This makes one whole stitch.

5 Repeat steps 1–4 for each stitch on the row. At the end of the row, switch your needle from one hand to the other and begin again on the other side of the fabric.

ERROR ALERT!

When learning to knit, errors will inevitably occur, and although imperfections can be the most charming part of a hand knit, here is how to avoid common mistakes.

First impressions

Avoid the common mistake of creating an extra stitch at the beginning of the row by making sure you are knitting into the correct loop.

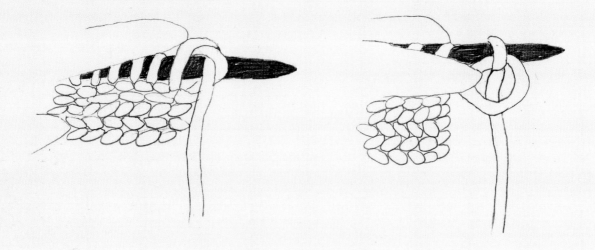

The knit stitch made on the last row can often be a bit loose and can look like the first loops on the needle to knit into.

Push the stitch down to reveal the correct loop to knit into.

No more, no less

The magic number of twenty stitches is a learning tool in itself. As the child knits, get them to count how many stitches they have at the end of each row.

One too many stitches? Knit 2 Together

The easiest quick fix is to knit two stitches together to get you back on an even keel. Pro-knitters will tell you this is cheating—but who cares!

This is ridiculously easy. All you do is carry out a knit stitch in exactly the same way as usual—just insert the needle through two loops instead of one.

PICKING UP THE PIECES

If there are one too few stitches, chances are it has dropped off the needle. A dropped stitch is the most urgent of errors as it can lead to a big, gaping hole in your knit. Teachers: be on hand with a crochet hook to pick up the stitches.

Lost and Found

If the stitch drops off the needle and you can still see the loop...

...quickly stick your needle back into the stitch, and move it back onto the left hand needle to be knitted. Phew!

Lost in the Wilderness

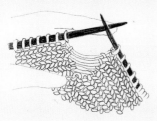

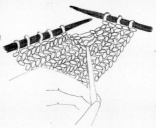

1 If your stitch has mysteriously disappeared, it will have unravelled down a number of rows. Unless you want a huge hole, you have to find the lost loop, and pick it back up. To be honest this is a right pain—so try to avoid it at all costs!

2 To do this properly you need to understand shape of the stitches —you will see that some look like v shapes and other's like bumps. Place the fabric in front of you so that the first stitch you want to make is a V (if it is a bump, turn the fabric over). Inset the crochet hook into the escaped loop from front to back and under the bar of yarn above it.

3 Hook the bar and pull it through the loop. Keep hold of this new loop you have formed.

4 Turn over the fabric, so that you will be making a V shape again, and repeat steps 2 and 3, until there are no bars of yarn left.

5 Transfer the loop from the crochet hook back onto the left needle. This whole process is tricky even for experienced knitters, and you may find that you have bumps where there should be 'V's, but it won't matter too much.

KEEP ON KNITTING!

With the 20 stitches you can start a small project that is quick to finish and will produce immediate results. A little change purse can be easily made from a folded rectangle of knitting (see page 74) and two small rectangles can give birth to a woolly monster (page 107)! If the knitster is a little more adventurous, they can try a full size scarf, but keep a pompom maker close by for those moments when they begin to get fidgety or frustrated. A change of yarn colour can also add interest...

From One Ball To Another

Here's how to make stripes or to introduce a new ball of yarn when one is all knit up. The best place to do this is at the end of a row.

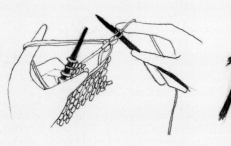
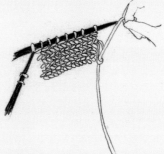
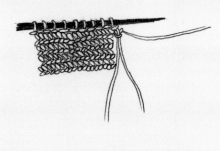

1 Cut the yarn leaving a 15 cm tail and place the beginning of the new ball of yarn with the tail. Hold them tightly together in your left hand.

2 Knit six stitches using the new yarn, keeping hold of both yarns in your left hand.

3 Stop for a moment and knot the two tails together firmly (but not too tight as you will undo it later).

4 Carry on knitting. When your knit is complete you can undo the joining knots and weave in all the ends to secure—this will give a bump-free finish (see Step 6 on opposite page).

CAST OFF

Once you are all 'knit up', you need to seal off the stitches, otherwise the whole thing is going to unwind. Sometimes referred to as 'binding off', casting off is basically securing the 'live' loops on the needle. It is much easier than casting on, and if you can master the knit stitch, you can also cast off.

• •

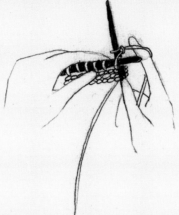

1 Knit the first two stitches on the row as normal.

2 Then insert the left hand needle into the first stitch (the one you made first, and furthest away from the needle point) on the right hand needle.

3 Lift the stitch over the second stitch (closest to the needle point) and off the end of the needle. Let go of the stitch—it has been cast off.

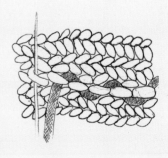

4 Knit another stitch as normal and then repeat steps 2 and 3.

5 Continue in this way until you have only one stitch left on the right hand needle. Cut the yarn with about 15 cm spare, push the end through the last loop, remove the needle and pull tight.

6 Think you've finished? To be done and dusted you must weave in all the 15 cm tails. All you do is thread the end through a yarn needle and on the back of the knit fabric pass the needle under the stitches until you can't go any further. Snip off the yarn close to the knit.

JOINED UP KNITTING

To make monsters and purses you will need to join together knit pieces. Here are a couple of simple ways to do so with a trusty yarn needle.

• •

Back-stitch

The back-stitch is strong and sturdy, what's more it's really quite easy.

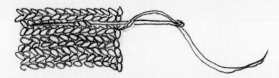

1 Place the pieces together and pin matching up the rows. Work at least one stitch in from the edges and make a stitch through both layers about 1 cm long. Pull the thread through.

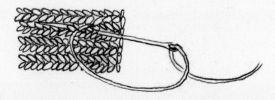

2 Now track back (hence the name), push the needle through the fabric midway between where you pushed the needle in and where it emerged on the last stitch. Make another 1 cm stitch, bringing the needle up about 0.5 cm further along than last time.

3 Repeat step 2 until you are done.

• •

Blanket stitch

The blanket stitch gives a decorative edge as well as a join, see page 34 for how to form this fancy number.

• •

FELTING

LIZ COOK

• •

Felting is one of the easiest crafts to master, and the results are amazingly effective. Get an old jumper, stick it in the washing machine on a hot wash, take it out, and the result is a very dense, warm material that will not fray when you cut it.

• •

1 Find a jumper or a scarf that you don't want anymore, and check the garment label to make sure it is wool. Only pure wool will be suitable for shrinking or 'fulling' in a washing machine. Occasionally mixed wool garments, e.g. 80 per cent wool 20 per cent nylon, will work. Check the label—if it says handwash only it should felt.

2 Lay the garment out and measure.

3 Place the garment in the washing machine, add two or three table spoons of delicate wool wash detergent and select hot wash.

4 If you are using a pure wool garment (such as lambswool) wash at 60° Celsius. Washing at a higher temperature may make the fabric too dense to sew easily. If it's a nylon mix, you can try at 70° Celsius. Angora and mohair felt very easily, so you may want to try a lower temperature first.

5 When the cycle has ended, remove the woollen piece and measure it again to check how much shrinkage has occurred. The maximum shrinkage you should be looking for is 50 per cent. Anywhere from 20 per cent to 40 per cent is desirable (depending on the texture that you're after). If it has shrunk successfully, then it is ready for use. If it has not shrunk much, then repeat the washing at a higher temperature.

6 Allow the garment to dry. Once fully dry you will be able to cut the fabric without the edges fraying.

how to recycle a sweater/jumper into... a multitude of household and personal accessories!!

mittens x 1 pair

leftovers = stuffing

tea cozy x 1

hot water bottle covers x 2

scarfs x 2 or 3

tips

Merino wool will not felt, as it is usually machine-washable.

Hand-knitted garments tend to shrink more than shop bought ones.

The bigger the jumper the more fabric there is to work with so go for XXL.

Start with a clean, dry jumper so there's no shrinkage in your final product after washing.

APPLIQUÉ

Appliqué is a sewing technique where fabric shapes are attached onto a base fabric. You are supposed to turn under the edges of your fabric shape for a neat look, but if you use felt or t-shirt fabric (iron on some interfacing to make it a bit stiffer), there is no need to do this.

HOW TO APPLIQUÉ

1 Draw the image onto the felt or t-shirt material.

2 Cut out, dab with a glue stick and position it on your work.

3 Now stitch into place with an overhand stitch. Insert the needle into the fabric next to your shape and bring it up just inside the shape. Use thread that matches the colour of the appliqué fabric or a contrasting one for a different effect.

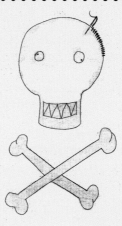

PAPIER-MÂCHÉ

KERRI SELLENS

Papier-mâché basically means 'mashed paper' in French. With bits of plain, boring old paper and a gloopy paste you can make solid 3-D structures. Layers of paper are built up over a mould, and the paper will take the shape of the object it covers. It is easy to do, but the process can take a number of days because you leave the paper to dry in between layers.

MATERIALS
- Newspaper, magazine, comic
- Plain flour
- Cup
- Wooden spoon
- Salt
- Saucepan, wooden spoon and mixing bowl
- Newspaper
- Object for a mould, cling film and Vaseline
- Paint brush (optional)

INSTRUCTIONS

Making the paste

1 Put 4 cups of water into the saucepan, place on the hob, and bring to the boil.

2 While you are waiting for the water to boil, mix together 1 cup of flour with 2 cups of water and stir well until there are no lumps.

3 When the water in the saucepan is boiling, turn down the heat and carefully add your flour and water mixture. Simmer for 2–3 minutes until smooth.

4 Add the salt and give the mixture a good stir.

5 Allow the paste to cool completely before you use it (this will take a few hours).

Choosing the mould

6 You need to cover your mould in Vaseline and then in cling film, unless you are using a balloon. Remember that you will need to remove the mould afterwards, and so cannot cover solid objects all over. Why not use a beaker or bowl to make fun containers for your bits and bobs?

Adding the paper

7 Tear your newspaper into small pieces; roughly 2x5 cm, but it's ok if they're all slightly different shapes and sizes.

8 Start applying the papier-mâché to the mould. Brush a little bit of paste onto one side of a paper strip and stick it onto the cling film. Brush some more paste over the top then do the same with another piece of paper.

9 Keep adding pieces of paper, overlapping and sticking them in different directions until the mould is covered.

10 Leave to dry in a warm place (a sunny windowsill is a good spot). Once it is completely dry to the touch, add a second layer of paper in the same way, and leave to dry. Repeat with a third, and final, layer.

11 To remove the mould from your creation, undo the ends of cling film inside the beaker/bowl and gently pull. The cling film should slowly slip away from the mould, taking the papier-mâché with it. Peel the cling film from the inside.

tips

It may be cheating, but using wallpaper paste works as well as making your own, and is much quicker!

Get your hands dirty—if you find using a paintbrush to paste the paper is a bit fiddly, just use your hands to smear on the paste.

Prepare your workstation! Big plastic bags laid out on the table will save it from getting soaked in paste (this works better than paper as it won't get soggy or stick to your papier-mâché).

POMPOM MANIA

Making pompoms can help keep interest when learning to knit, but these soft fuzzy balls are also just cool things in themselves. You can buy cheap plastic pompom makers from knitting shops—these are a good investment if you intend to make many, and they are so simple even three and four year olds can use them, with a little help! They come in different sizes—all you have to do is follow the instructions.

But, why buy something if you can make it, right? Here's how to craft your own pompom maker whilst recycling a cardboard box.

MATERIALS

- Cardboard box—the thickness of a shoebox works well
- Set of compasses
- Pencil
- Ruler
- Yarns
- Sharp scissors

INSTRUCTIONS

1 Take apart the box so that you can lay it down flat and place the pencil in the compass.

2 The pompom maker is made up of two cardboard discs (like flat doughnuts with a hole in the middle) of the same size. For each disc you need to draw two circles inside one another. From the table select one of the sizes:

Pompom size	Radius of outer circle	Radius of inner circle
Small	2 cm	0.8 cm
Medium	3 cm	1.2 cm
Large	4 cm	1.6 cm
Extra large	5 cm	2 cm

3 The radius is the distance between the centre of the circle and the edge: this is the distance that you set the compass to. So for the medium pompom, for example, use a ruler to set the distance between the compass point and the pencil tip to 3 cm.

4 Tighten up the screw on the compass and draw two circles on the cardboard.

5 Now reset the compass to the radius of the inner circle. So again, using the medium pompom as an example, 1.2 cm between the compass point and the pencil tip. Place the compass point on the centre point again to draw the inner circle. Repeat on the second circle.

6 Now use the ruler to draw two lines close together from the centre to the edge of the circle, like a thin sliver of pie (fig. 1). Repeat on the other circle.

7 Cut out along the purple lines shown in fig. 1, to make the cardboard discs.

8 To make the pompom place the discs on top of one another so that the slits are in the same position.

9 Now wrap yarn around the disc, using the slit to get into the centre (fig. 2). You can use a couple of balls of yarn at once, holding the strands together to speed up the process. If you use different colours you will get a speckled ball! You can bend the disc to make it easier to wrap (fig. 3).

10 You need to wrap and wrap until the cardboard is covered with many layers, until the centre hole is nearly filled with yarn and only a small hole remains (fig. 4). Cut the ends of yarn and secure by pulling under a few wraps.

11 This bit is a bit tricky and best done with two people. Starting at the slit, wiggle the scissors in between the two layers of yarn. Cut through all strands of yarn all the way around. One way to do this is to place the yarn-covered disc on a flat surface and get someone to hold a glass jar, cup, etc. on top whilst you cut around (fig. 5).

12 Cut a 30 cm or so strand of yarn and pull it between the two discs. Wrap it around the yarn in the centre (fig. 6) and tie as tightly as you can. Wrap the yarn around again and tie securely with a couple of knots.

13 Now you can remove the discs and fluff up the pompom. If it looks a bit uneven, trim any stray strands.

tip

Stick on paper-circle eyes for a pompom pal!

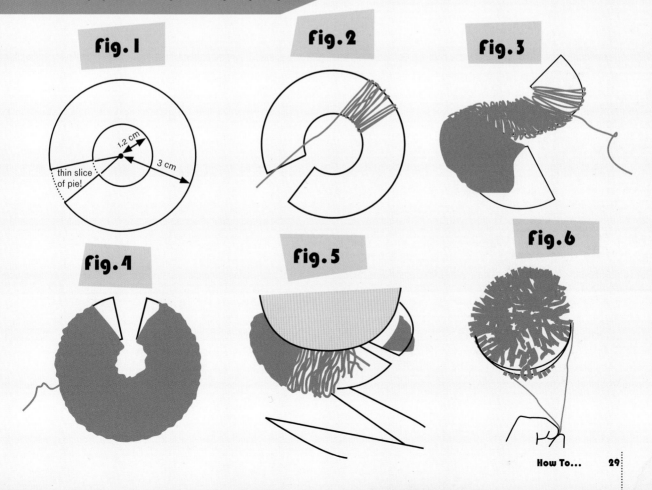

fig. 1

1.2 cm

3 cm

thin slice of pie!

fig. 2

fig. 3

fig. 4

fig. 5

fig. 6

SEW SIMPLE

No matter what age you are, the important thing about sewing is to remember that it is essentially pretty simple. Think of the actual act of sewing stitches as just a way of joining together two pieces of fabric, just as you would join two pieces of paper using glue or tape.

THE SEWING KIT

Material Gain

Going into a fabric shop is really quite an amazing experience! However, with such a variety of materials available it can be rather mesmerising. From cottons and silks to towelling and tulle, there are all kinds of textures, colours and patterns. At all costs when starting out, stay away from stretchy fabrics (just about OK for the Bobby Dazzler Beanbag Buddy)—they are nothing but trouble! For the purposes of this book, the projects will specify what fabrics to use, but on the whole stick to fairly sturdy cotton as it is easy to sew and easy to see the grain (more about this below).

Don't forget that you can sew with old clothes too. Keep a pile of unwanted skirts and shirts for small projects. Felt is great for adding embellishments, as it won't fray, and can be bought or made from old jumpers. Interfacing is another useful fabric—it is used to stiffen and thicken fabric. You can get iron-on fusible interfacing (does what you'd expect!).

The sales assistants in a fabric shop will always know their stuff—so just ask!

Thread

Sewing threads most commonly come in cotton and polyester. The trick is to look for the phrase "all-purpose"—you can't go wrong! Just pick a colour to match your fabric. You can use embroidery threads for decorative stitching—but it's not for machines!

A needle for every occasion

Get a set with a variety of lengths and thicknesses, so you'll have a need a needle for every thread.

For sewing through woven fabric you need sharp points (you can also get ballpoint needles—which work on dreaded stretchy fabrics).

Cut it up

Dressmakers have their own special scissors. For the purposes of this book they aren't needed, but you will need a good sharp pair, and adults should therefore cut out fabric for younger kids.

Pin it down

Dressmaker's pins keep things together. The ones with coloured ends are better for kids as they are easier to see and pick up.

Chalk to me

Tailor's chalk is useful for drawing around patterns. It comes in a variety of colours and can be brushed off. You can also sometimes find fabric markers, which are designed so that the ink either washed off, or magically disappears! You could also just use a regular pencil, as normally the pattern lines can't be seen once sewn.

Machine Scene

Many of the projects in this book can be hand-sewn, except for when it says "sewing machine" in the materials section. If you have a sewing machine, take some time to get to know it! Read the manual and practise threading-up and loading the bobbin.
From about age ten children can use a machine to sew straight lines, but always accompanied by an adult. If you don't have a machine, ask around: lots of people have one gathering dust. And if you have never sewn on a machine before: get the owner to give you a tutorial! This book does not explain the many ins and outs of machine sewing so if you are learning from scratch you will need to find another source to help you along the way.

Fancy notions

Notions are what you get from a haberdashery! Still not getting it? In other words, all the extra exciting bits and bobs, like buttons, ribbon and lace. Mmmm!

Other things

Some of the sewing projects in this book with require an iron. Buy a seam ripper so that when you make mistakes you can un-pick them with minimum fuss. And a tape measure for, um, measuring.

● ●

STUFF TO KNOW BEFORE YOU SEW

● ●

Knowing right from wrong

Yep, there is a wrong side and right side to fabric. This is one of the first things to get to grips with. The right side is the one you want to show to the world, and the wrong side will be hidden on the inside of your creation. Take a good look at the fabric. On printed and textured fabric it is easy to tell which is which. If you can't tell, don't worry. Both sides must look so similar that it doesn't matter which side you use.

You will come across the phrase 'with right sides together' a lot: just place the designated right sides touching together so that the wrong side is facing you. Oh, and the phrase 'turn right side out' just means to adjust your sewing so that the right side of the fabric is showing on the outside—where it belongs.

The grain of the fabric

A little more tricky this one! Take another good look at your (non-stretchy!) fabric. You should be able to see the thousands of lines of threads that are woven together to make the material. The threads run lengthwise and crosswise, or up and down and from side to side, at a 90 degree angle to each other. This is also known as the warp and the weft (from 'weft' to right!). When you position a rectangular pattern piece for example the edges need to line up with these lines. This is easy when you have a whole piece of fabric cut from a roll as the lines that make up the grain will run parallel to the finished un-cut edge (also known as the selvage, by the way). However, when you have a scrap with no finished edge, you will have to look carefully to see the grain.

● ●

THREADY, STEADY, GO!

● ●

Thread up

Cut a length of thread about 30–40 cm long: not much longer or it will get tangled up. Angle the thread through the eye of the needle and pull about 10 cm of the thread through. Tie two or three knots at the other end and you're away.

● ●

One thread or two

Normally you want to sew with just one thickness of thread, but if the instructions tell you to double up the thread, here's what you do. Cut about 60 cm of thread and thread the needle. Pull half the yarn through until the two ends are together and knot them both. Double up the thread when you sew on a button to make it quicker!

Stitch it

Sewing at last. Welcome to the stitches themselves:

Straight or Running Stitch

This is the standard broken-dash stitch. Just run your needle in and out through the fabric, in a linear fashion. N.B. When instructions in this book simply say 'sew', this is the one you want to use!

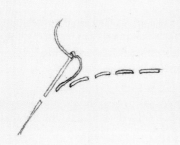

Basting Stitch

Exactly the same as the Running Stitch, except that the lengths of the stitches are exceptionally long. This is used to hold two pieces of fabric in place before running them through the sewing machine.

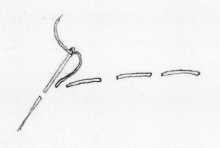

Backstitch

Backstitch is the strongest hand stitch and is used to imitate machine stitches. Work backstitch from right to left. Bring the needle up from the back of the fabric, and then make the first stitch by pushing the needle into the fabric behind (to the right of) the thread, and bringing it back up in front of (to the left of) the thread, by the same distance. Keep repeating the action, bringing the needle back to the previous stitch each time, to create a continuous line.

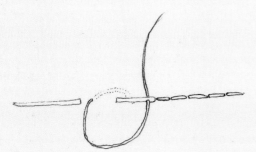

Safe and secure

You must remember to knot or sew a few stitches on the spot before you cut the thread, otherwise the stitches will come undone. On a machine, you may have a backstitch function: use this at the beginning and end of each line you sew to secure.

Machine Club

On a sewing machine you can set the stitch to a straight running stitch, but you can also alter the length of the stitch. You want to set the length to 2.5 for regular stitches. Again, when instructions in this book simply say 'sew', this is what you do.

BEHIND THE SEAMS

Seam-stress

Seams are the bedrock of constructive sewing, but don't stress! It's just joining one bit of fabric to another. They are worked on the wrong side of the fabric. The easiest way to understand seams is with a little experiment. Take two rectangles of fabric (cut along the grainlines of course) and place them right sides together (just look how down with the lingo you are!). Place a few pins through the two layers to hold them together. Now sew a straight line (either a running stitch or straight stitch on a machine) roughly 1 cm in from the edge securing the stitches at each end. Un-pin and open right side out. You joined two pieces with a seam.

Seam allowance

'Seam allowance' is the term used for the distance between the edge of the fabric and where you sew (so in the above example you stitched a seam with a 1 cm seam allowance).

Top-notch seams

When you progress onto curved seams (not as scary as they sound), you may have to 'notch' the seam allowance before turning the fabric right side out. This means to cut small V shapes out of the fabric. You cut from the edge close to the line of stitching, but not touching. In this book it will always be explained when and where you need to do this.

OVER THE TOP!

Top it off

When you sew on the right side of the fabric as when making a hem, it is sometimes referred to as topstitch, but it is just a straight or running stitch that you can see.

Hem

A hem is a neat edge on fabric. It is constructed by turning over the fabric edge twice so that the rough bit can't be seen. When you need to do this in a project you will be reminded of what to do.

Here are some more stitches that you use on the right side of the fabric (and these babies have to be hand-stitched):

Overhand stitch

This is the little stitch number you use to appliqué: see page 26.

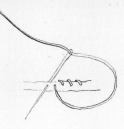

Whipstitch

This little number joins two edges on the right sides of the fabric. Join the thread onto the fabric and hold the fabric with one hand. Pass the needle from one side to the other. Bring the needle over the top of the join and pass the needle through the fabric in the same direction as before.

In Stitches
Additional handmade stitches that are used for decoration such as embroidery:

Split stitch

This stitch creates a continuous running like, with no breaks at all. It's good for basic embroidery, as you can use it to follow any line drawing you like. All you need to do, is make a small stitch, and then bring the needle up for the next stitch through the centre of the thread of the previous stitch, 'splitting' it.

Chain Stitch

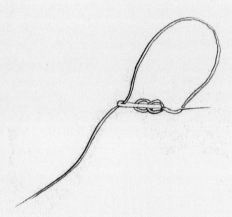

Pull your thread up through the fabric and re-insert next to where the needle just exited. Instead of pulling the thread through into a stitch, leave the thread in a loose loop. Bring your needle up under this loop and through it to make your next stitch. The result is a continuous stitch that can look a little like the split stitch.

Blanket Stitch

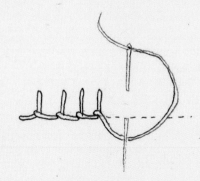

This utilitarian and aesthetically pleasing stitch can be used along the edge of your fabric to make visible chunky stitches in a contrasting colour. Work from left to right. Bring the needle up from the wrong side of the fabric, make a diagonal stitch, and when you bring your needle up to make the next stitch, come up under the first one, pulling the thread down to make a right angle.

BUTTON UP!

Here is a quick explanation of how to sew on a button. There are actually a ton of different techniques for this simple task. But here is the basic principle.

1 Thread a needle and double up the thread.

2 Choose the spot where you want the button and starting on the right side of the fabric make a little stitch. Pull the thread through to the knot.

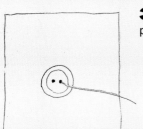

3 Push the needle through one of the holes in the button, from back to front, and push the button up to the fabric.

4 Push the needle through the other hole and through the fabric to the back.

5 Bring the needle back to the right side of the fabric through the first hole and back to the wrong side through the second hole. Keep repeating this action until the button is secure. Make a few little stitches on the wrong side (behind the button) to secure and cut the thread.

TEENY TALENTS

AGES 3+

1

ANIMAL SNAPPERS

LOGLIKE

Loglike's quirky animal snapper toys are made from regular clothes pegs and can be clipped onto pencil ends, pull-cords and curtains: anywhere you can think of. Clip them onto sticks to make puppets, or snap onto a metal bolt and move them around with a magnet. Snap-tastic!

MATERIALS
- Hinged wooden pegs
- PVA glue and a small brush
- Sharp craft knife and cutting mat (or old piece of floor lino
- Scissors
- A pencil or fine pen
- Interesting old fabric
- Corrugated card (can be found on some cardboard boxes and packaging)
- Small scrap of coloured card (for the elephant)
- Beads or lentils for the eyes (2 per animal)

INSTRUCTIONS

1 Photocopy and enlarge, or re-draw to scale, an animal template and cut out the rectangle surrounding the animal.

2 Draw around the rectangle on corrugated card and cut out.

3 Cut a piece of fabric a little bigger than the cardboard rectangle.

4 Paint PVA onto one side of the card: a thin, even layer is best. Paint it quickly so it doesn't dry and place the fabric onto the glue. Press the fabric down very gently so it makes contact all over the cardboard, but the glue doesn't show through. Leave to dry.

5 Now carefully cut out the animal shapes from the paper template. Place them on top of the fabric-covered card, and draw around the shapes. Cut the animals out using a sharp craft knife. If the cardboard isn't too thick, you might be able to use scissors for this.

6 If you're making the elephant or the giraffe, trace and cut out the ear templates from contrasting fabric. Cut a slot in the card animal as shown on the template with the craft knife. Push the fabric into the slit. Fix it to the back of the card with PVA glue, leaving the fabric ear to flap around on the front.

7 Glue on the eyes. The elephant also has tusks: cut these from coloured card and glue on with PVA glue.

8 Glue the fabric covered cardboard animal shapes to the pegs with lots of PVA glue. You need two animal shapes per peg, so that there's a front and a back. Take care to place the peg slightly above the bottom of the animal, as shown in the template drawing. This will help the animals stand up well on their feet. Lay the animal down flat and place a heavy object on top so that they dry in the right position. Leave to dry thoroughly.

TEMPLATES

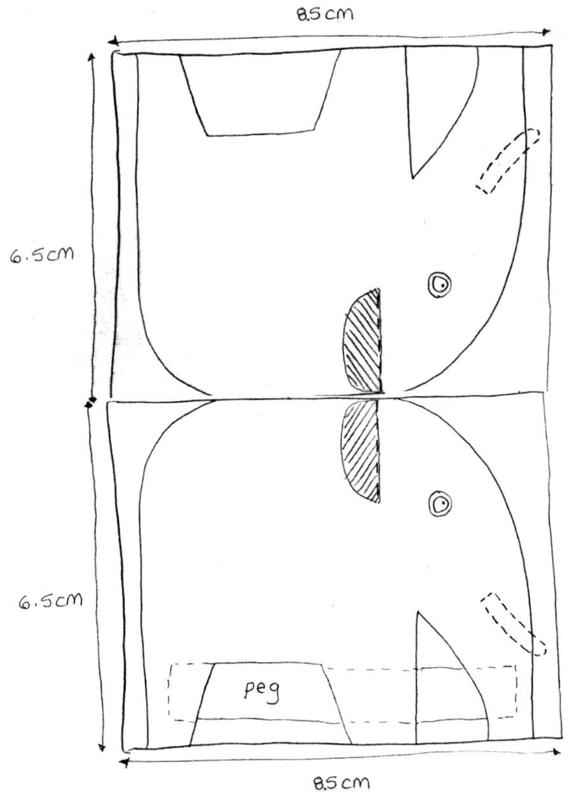

8.5 cm

6.5 cm

6.5 cm

peg

8.5 cm

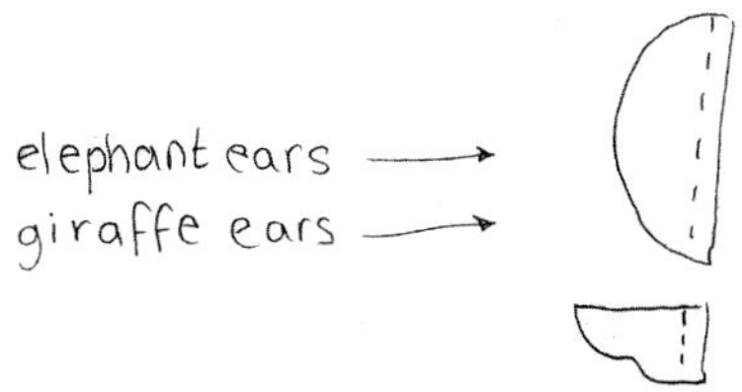

elephant ears →

giraffe ears →

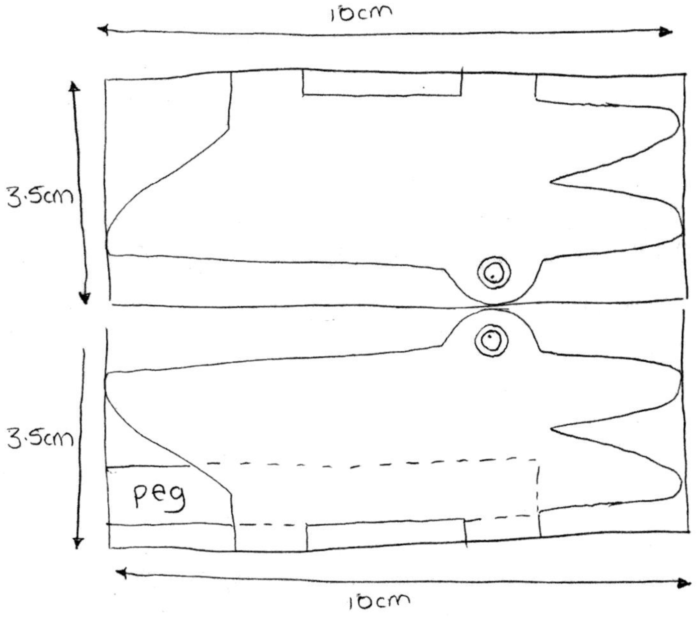

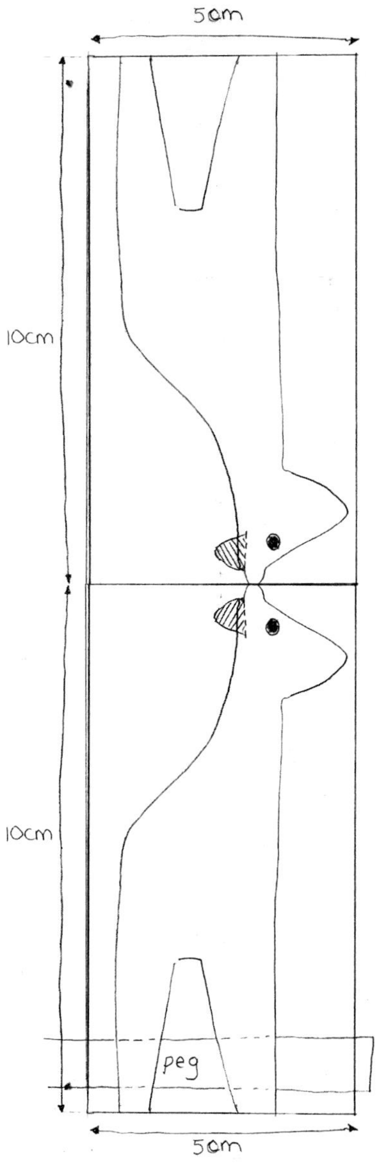

5 cm

10 cm

10 cm

peg

5 cm

10 cm

3.5 cm

3.5 cm

peg

10 cm

2

A VERY HUNGRY PUPPET

TRATINCICA SLAVICEK

Old woolly jumpers can be used in many crafty ways—one of which is to turn them into crawling caterpillars. This simple puppet is especially popular with small children. With a little bit of grown-up help, even three year olds can make their very own caterpillar, and then have fun crawling, nibbling, wiggling around.

MATERIALS

- Fleece or felt in different shades of green and yellow (to make felt from old jumpers see page 25)
- 1 big pompom (see page 28 for how to make your own)
- Thick thread or wool
- 1 thick blunt needle
- Scissors
- Non-toxic fabric glue
- Multi-purpose strong glue
- Felt in different colours
- 1 pipe-cleaner
- 2 wooden beads
- Small amounts of felt in different colours for eyes and mouth
- Wooden rods or chopsticks approx. 15 cm long
- Sandpaper

INSTRUCTIONS

1 Make a pompom by following the instructions on page 28. The larger the pompom the larger your caterpillar will be.

2 Cut the felt into strips roughly the same width as the pompom and cut the strips into squares. Put several felt squares ontop of each other and make them more rounded by cutting off the corners in a curve.

3 Thread a blunt needle with about 1 metre of thick, strong thread. Double the thread over and tie a knot at the end. Push the needle through the centre of the felt circles. If the needle does not go through easily make a small hole in the middle of each one with sharp scissors.

4 When all the felt pieces are on the thread, sew the thread through the centre of the pompom. Pull the thread so that the caterpillar is quite tight, and tie a couple of knots to secure.

5 Cut eyes and mouth out of small contrasting pieces of felt, and glue them on the caterpillar's head (the pompom).

6 Cut a pipe-cleaner in half and stick a wooden bead at the end of each length. Push the other ends into the pompom.

7 Sand down one end of the rods (where you will be holding) and attach the ends to the body. Push one rod into the bottom of the head and one further along the body. Secure with a few dabs of glue and leave to dry.

8 Set up a screen—you can make a simple one by hanging a sheet or towel over the back of a chair. Make the caterpillar crawl across the top by moving the two sticks together and apart. You can make him wiggle, curl himself in a knot or scratch his head with his tail... have fun!

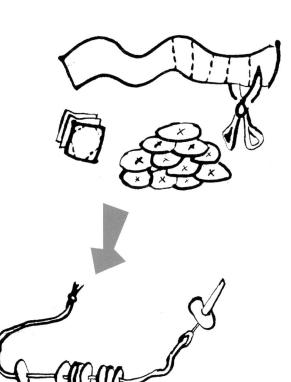

Caterpillar

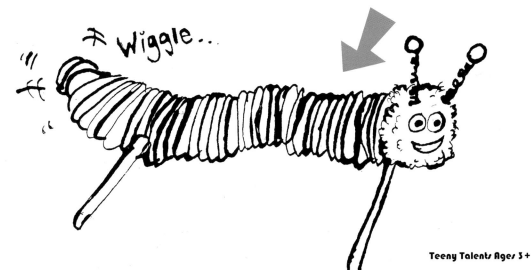

Wiggle...

3

MAGNETIC BUTTON SPIDER

RACHEL MOGFORD

Scare your friends with this creepy spider that can crawl up and down the curtains... on its own!

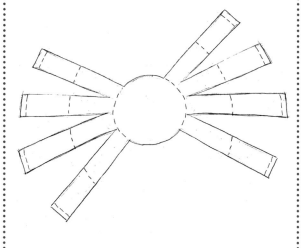

MATERIALS
- Black paper
- 1 medium sized black button
- 2 small magnets
- Double sided tape or PVA glue
- Paper scissors

INSTRUCTIONS

1 Cut out a spider shape from the black paper. Use the template as a guide, making it bigger or smaller depending on the size of your button. The button will be the spider's body.

2 Use double-sided tape or PVA glue to stick the button to the centre of your spider shape.

3 Turn the spider over. Stick one of the magnets to the centre of the paper spider (underneath the button). You need to be careful which way you glue the magnet. Touch together the surfaces of the magnets: two of the surfaces of the magnets will pull together forcefully. You put glue on the surface that is not attached to the other magnet.

4 Turn the spider over again so the button faces upwards, and make folds in each of the spider's legs to form its knees and feet.

5 You can now control the spider with the other magnet. Hold the spider on one side of a curtain (or any thin surface) and the magnet in the same place on the other side. Move the magnet, and watch as the spider moves with it. Creepy!

TEMPLATE

4

POP ART CARD

VICTORIA WOODCOCK

Surprise your friends with a pop-up card that will really stand out!

MATERIALS
- 2 pieces of card the same size—cut a piece of A4 (8.3×11.7 in) in half
- Glue stick
- Scissors
- Pencil
- Ruler
- Bits of card, paper, magazines, etc., for the pop-up design

INSTRUCTIONS

1 Work on the design that will pop-up. The final design shouldn't be any bigger than 11 cm across and 9 cm high. Cut out letters of paper or from magazines and stick them on a rectangle of coloured card to make a card like this one. You can also use images cut out of newspapers or printed off the computer—just stick them onto card before you cut them out. One idea is to cut out an image of a pop-star or cartoon character and make a speech bubble for your message.

2 Fold both pieces of card in half.

3 On one piece of card, find the centre of the folded edge and make a small pencil mark. Draw a line either side of this mark at right angles to the edge. The lines should be about 2 cm long and about 2–3 cm apart (fig. 1).

4 With the card still folded, cut along the lines. Push the card between the lines to make a pop-up box (fig. 2).

5 Stick your pop-up design to one side of the pop-up box (fig. 3).

6 Glue all over the other folded piece of card and attach the back of the pop-up part to it.

7 Decorate the front of the card.

tip

More complex designs can be made with more than one pop-up box. Make boxes of different sizes (cutting longer or shorter line, but always two the same length) for a 3-D extravaganza!

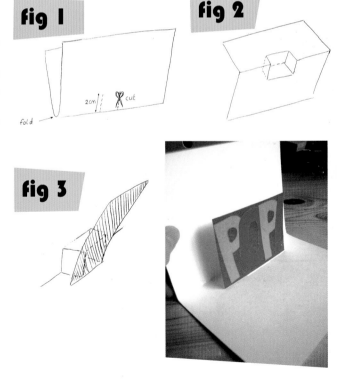

fig 1

2 cm   cut

fold

fig 2

fig 3

5

MR CYLINDER HEAD

JIM MORRIS

Jim Morris's puppets in this book are all inspired by The Muppets—they all have cheeky personalities and gift of the gab. Make his other two puppets on pages 48 and 62, grab a couple of friends and host a talk show!

MATERIALS

- 2 sheets of thin A3 card (11.7×16.5 in)
- Some scraps of thin card (in the same or different colours)
- Lots of ribbons—a couple of reels of the cheap parcel wrapping variety
- Sellotape or Scotch tape
- Scissors
- Glue stick

INSTRUCTIONS

1 Tightly roll an A3 card sheet to make a long thin tube. Secure it with small pieces of tape (fig. 1).

2 Curve another A3 sheet of card around more loosely to make a cylinder and secure it with small pieces of tape for the head (fig. 2).

3 Cut all the way around the cylinder to create two parts—one smaller than the other. This will become the jaw (fig. 3).

4 Fix the upper part of the head to the narrow tube with two strips of tape at the top and bottom. The top piece of tape should be folded into the tube to secure it (fig. 4).

5 Now add the jaw to the bottom half of the puppet, using a single piece of sellotape to stick the top of the cylinder to the narrow tube so that it acts as a 'hinge'—enabling the jaw to move (fig. 5).

6 From your scraps of card, cut out a triangle for the nose, two circles for the eyes and two ovals for the ears. Cut out more triangles for teeth (fig. 6+7).

7 Fold the nose in half, so it stands out and stick it on with sellotape.

8 Glue on the eyes, ears and teeth or use Sellotape or Scotch tape (fig. 7).

9 Tape ribbons inside the top of the cylinder for hair.

6

CREEPY CRAWLY WORMERY

CAMILLA STACEY

What better thing to do on a rainy day than to go looking for worms! Discover the fascinating underground world of worms with a DIY wormery. Worms are the one creepy crawly gardeners always like to see (unlike slugs) because they help keep the soil in tip-top condition. Worms don't eat living plants, so they won't damage anything in the garden, but they do like to eat a lot of dead plants and leaves. Just like any other animal that eats, worms also pooh! Worm pooh is really good for plants and the tunnels that worms make through the soil means that the soil will be full of air and not all squashed down.

MATERIALS
• Worms!
• Big clean glass jar with a lid
• Sand
• Soil
• Some grass/leaves
• A nail and hammer to make holes in the jar lid
• Spoon
• Thick black paper
• Blu-tac or plasticine

INSTRUCTIONS

1 Before you find any worms, you need to prepare their home. Worms need to breathe just like us, so make some holes in the lid of your jar (don't use a jar with a glass lid!). To do so, stick the lid to a workbench (or a big thick catalogue—anything that no-one will mind there being holes in!) with a bit of Blu-tac or Plasticine. Hammer a nail into the lid, and remove again, to create about five or six holes.

2 Use a spoon to fill the jar with a layer of sand about 2.5 cm thick. Follow with a similar sized layer of soil. Keep adding layers of sand and soil for a stripy effect until you reach roughly 2.5 cm from the top of the jar.

3 Worms like it if the ground is damp, so add a little bit of water to the jar. The sand and soil should be soggy, but don't flood the jar because worms don't want to live underwater!

4 Put some grass and dead leaves on top of the earth—this is what the worms will eat. You could also add vegetable peelings or even old coffee grinds.

5 Now for the fun bit—finding some worms in the garden! Remember to ask whoever owns the garden if you can dig in the soil as you might accidentally dig up something important. You will find more worms on a rainy day, and good places to look are under plant pots and in compost heaps. If you can't find any worms at all, you could buy some from a fishing shop instead.

6 When you have about ten worms, put them into the jar and make sure you put the lid on tightly—this is very important unless you want worms all over your house!

7 Worms like it best when it is dark, so wrap some thick black paper around the jar to trick them into thinking its night. Leave the jar in a cool, dark place for about a week.

8 Take the paper off to see what the worms have been doing. Look at the tunnels the worms have made through the sand and soil. The food you left on the top of the soil will have disappeared, as the worms will have taken it down into their tunnels.

9 When you have finished looking at the worms make sure you put them back in the garden, or onto the compost heap. Worms are really helpful in the garden so next time you see one, be nice to it!

'TALKING HEAD' PUPPET ...

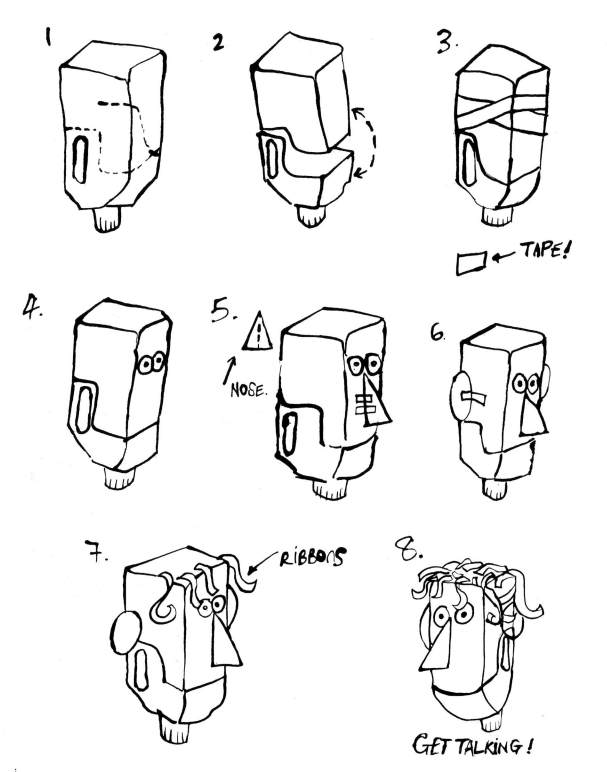

1.

2.

3.

▭ ← TAPE!

4.

5. ⚠ ↑ NOSE.

6.

7. → RIBBONS

8.

GET TALKING!

7
TALKING HEAD PUPPET

JIM MORRIS

From milk container to chatter-box: another yakking puppet for your collection!

• •

MATERIALS
- 1 empty 2 litre (4 pint) plastic milk container (make sure it's clean and dry).
- Brown parcel tape
- Scissors or a craft knife
- Coloured card
- White label stickers (optional)
- Thin card
- Lots of ribbons—a couple of reels of the cheap parcel wrapping variety

• •

INSTRUCTIONS

1 Turn the container upside down with its cap on, and carefully cut along three sides using scissors or a craft knife to give your puppet a moving jaw (figs. 1+2).

2 Wrap the parcel tape around the container to create a 'skin' (fig. 3). If you tape over the jaw, just use a craft knife to cut it again. Don't worry about wrinkles—it's all part of the character!

3 Using label stickers or coloured card, cut two big circles out for eyes, and draw a black circle in the middle (fig. 4). Stick these on (if you're using card, just tape them on with sellotape).

4 Cut out a triangle from the coloured card and fold it down the middle. Stick it on with sellotape to make a nose (fig. 5).

5 Cut out two ovals and stick them on for the ears (fig. 6).

6 Cut coloured ribbons to lengths of approximately 20 or 30 cm, and stick them to the top of the container to give your puppet a hairstyle. To make curls, hold scissors shut and run the metal edge along the ribbon quickly (fig. 7). Boing!

7 Hold the handle at the back of the puppet's head, and place your other hand on the top of the puppets head, when you move your hand, the puppet gets talking (fig. 8)!

8

THE CEREAL BOX THEATRE

TONI CHILD

A quick and easy way to put on a show—great fun for all ages!

· ·

MATERIALS
- Cereal box
- Plain paper
- Brightly coloured paper in different colours (wrapping paper works best)
- Felt tip pens
- Pencils
- Scissors
- Glue stick
- Ruler
- Sellotape or Scotch tape

· ·

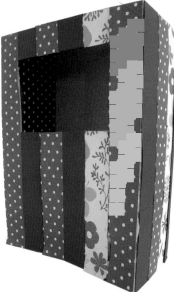

INSTRUCTIONS

1 Cut the flaps off the open end of an empty cereal box

2 Mark three points about 3 cm from the top of the box and from either side. Use a ruler to join up the points to form a rectangle. Cut it out.

3 Cut another rectangle about the same size on the other side of the box at the bottom, so that you can stick your hand in.

4 Cut strips of colourful paper about 1 cm wide. Using the glue stick, paste these over the box, to make it bright and exciting.

5 Draw some characters for your show on a piece of paper. Glue the paper onto the leftover card from your cut-out rectangles, and stick the characters onto the tops of pencils with Sellotape or Scotch tape.

6 You're ready to put on your show!

tips

You could also decorate your puppet show with stickers, pictures cut out from comics or magazines—anything at all really.

Make sure you stick your puppets on the unsharpened end of the pencil, so you can still you use them for colouring in!

You could also use Peg People (see page 52) as puppets in your theatre.

9

PEBBLE PALS

CAMILLA STACEY

Turn pebbles into helpful creatures for your garden: hedgehogs eat slugs and other pests and ladybirds eat aphids that damage plants.

· ·

MATERIALS

• Smooth pebbles—large or small, it's up to you Find them on the beach and near rivers, but don't take too many from nature. You can also buy them from a garden centre.
• Small paintbrushes
• Poster or acrylic paints
• Wobbly eyes (optional)
• Clear varnish
• Pot of water

· ·

INSTRUCTIONS

1 Scrub the stones with soap and water so they are nice and clean. Leave them in a warm dry place to dry out —this will take a while, so do it the day before you begin painting.

2 All you need to do is paint the top of the pebbles. Cover the table in newspaper and keep a pot of water to one side so that you can rinse the paintbrush thoroughly to remove all the paint before changing colours. To dry the paintbrush after rinsing, dab in on the newspaper.

3 For the ladybird, paint the front third of the pebble black and the remaining two thirds of the pebble red. Leave the paint to dry for half an hour or so and add black spots and a line to show where the wings are. Add white dots for eyes, or if you plan to keep your pet indoors, stick on some wobbly eyes!

4 For the hedgehog, paint the first third of the pebble light brown or yellow and the remaining two thirds dark brown. When the paint has dried, use black paint to add spiky spines, eyes and a nose.

5 Leave the paint to dry. If you want your pebble pets to live in the garden you need to add a layer of varnish to protect them from the rain. Use a clean and dry paintbrush and cover the painted area in varnish.

tip

What other creatures could you paint on your stones that would be helpful in the garden? How about a bumble bee or an ant?

10

PEG PEOPLE

CAMILLA STACEY

They're anything but wooden!

●●●●●●●●●●●●●●●●●●●●●●●●●●●●●●

MATERIALS
- 'Dolly' clothes pegs—you can pay a lot for these in fashionable 'shabby chic' shops, but look in hardware stores and pound shops for cheap ones
- Pipe cleaners
- PVA glue
- Paintbrush
- Scissors
- Felt-tip pens
- Scraps of fabric, paper and ribbons for clothes
- Knitting yarn for hair
- Plasticine (optional)

●●●●●●●●●●●●●●●●●●●●●●●●●●●●●●

INSTRUCTIONS

1 Start to see your peg like a person! The ball at the top is the head, with the two peg legs at the other end, but you need to give your peg person some arms! Take a pipe cleaner and wrap one end around the 'neck' of the peg a couple of times and bend it out to the side to form an arm. Repeat with a second pipe cleaner to form an arm on the other side.

2 You might find it easier to draw on the face if you stick the legs into a ball of Plasticine. Use felt-tip pens to draw eyes, nose and mouth onto the rounded 'head' end of the peg. You can draw a different face on each side!

3 Cut short strands of woolly yarn for the hair— between 10 and 15 cm depending on the desired length. Paint a thin layer of PVA glue onto the top of the head and stick on the hair one strand at a time. Add more glue as you add more strands—it will dry clear so it doesn't matter if it looks a bit messy.

For complicated hairstyles, like a bun, you might need to make a little 'wig', gluing together pieces of yarn first before sticking it onto the peg.

4 Leave the glue to dry—you could work on the arms and faces of another peg doll while the hair is drying.

5 Give the hair some style! You can give your person a haircut or add plaits. Don't tug too hard or you might pull the hair off.

6 Clothes will add colour and personality to your peg people. For tops, cut out squares or circles of fabric and make a hole in the centre to pop the head through. Use PVA glue to stick the fabric together under the arms. Wrap a rectangle of fabric, foil or paper around for a skirt and tie a piece of ribbon around. You can also paint the legs for trousers. Add paper hats, sequins, leaves and anything else you can think of.

Peg People

FRONT / BACK
FACE

plasticine

< 10 - 15cm

GLUE

ADD ! AT A TIME

tips

Here are some ideas for Peg People characters

Princess Peggy
Use long yellow wool for hair. Cut a circle of felt out for a top and make a hole in the middle of the circle for her head to go through. Add second circle of felt and glue the middle of this to the middle of the peg for a skirt.

The Abominable Peg Man
Make extra-long monstrous arms by joining several pipe cleaners together. Cover the whole peg with furry fabric and draw glowing red eyes onto the head.

Adam and Eve
Use long brown yarn for hair and stick leaves from the garden on in the right places as fig leaves. Tie yarn to the pipe cleaners for a beard.

11

EGGHEADS

CAMILLA STACEY

Grow something you can eat in something you have eaten!

• •

MATERIALS
• Empty egg shells
• Cotton wool
• Cress seeds
• Permanent marker or felt-tip pens
• Egg cup

• •

INSTRUCTIONS

1 Crack open an uncooked egg by tapping the top of the egg on the side of a bowl. Catch the egg in the bowl (you can use it to make a cake) and a big part of the eggshell should have stayed in one piece. Alternatively, eat a soft-boiled dippy egg, and use the shell you have eaten from.

2 Gently rinse out the empty eggshell and place it in an eggcup to keep it steady. Draw a face on the egg with felt tips (fig. 1).

3 Fill the shell with damp cotton wool (fig. 2).

4 Scatter cress seeds on top of the cotton wool.

5 Place your egghead in a warm sunny place like a window sill. Keep the cotton wool damp by sprinkling with water every day and soon green hair will start to sprout.

6 The best bit is that you can eat the cress hair! Try a classic egg and cress sandwich—which means breaking some more eggs!

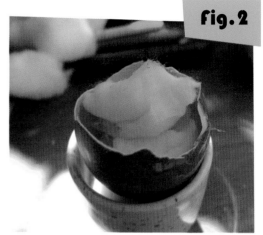

fig. 1

fig. 2

2 MINS!

+ ANOTHER 2 MINS

WOW!

PLAY DOUGH
SPARKLY

12

SPARKLE AND SHINE PLAY DOUGH

ZOE BIBBY

Whip up your own special shimmery play dough in the microwave using ordinary kitchen ingredients.

MATERIALS

- 1 cup plain flour
- ½ cup salt
- 2 teaspoons cream of tartar
- 1 tablespoon cooking oil
- 1 cup water
- Glitter
- Few drops of food colouring
- Glass mixing bowl
- Wooden spoon
- Chopping board (optional)
- Microwave safe bowl
- Microwave
- Airtight container

INSTRUCTIONS

1 Place all the ingredients except the glitter into a glass mixing bowl and mix thoroughly with a wooden spoon.

2 Place the bowl in the microwave and cook on high (full power) for 2 minutes.

3 Remove the bowl from the microwave and stir thoroughly, mixing in all the thickened bits from the edge of the bowl. Return to the microwave and cook for a further 2 minutes.

4 Stir again thoroughly. By now the whole mixture should have a dense, thick consistency. If not, cook again for 1 minute at a time, stirring well between each minute.

5 Once the dough forms a pliable ball which holds together and leaves the side of the bowl clean, it is ready. Turn the ball out onto a chopping board or clean surface to cool down. Watch out, it will be very hot!

6 When it is thoroughly cool, sprinkle on as much glitter as you like and knead it into the dough. The dough will keep well in an airtight container.

7 Now start sculpting!

tip

The sparkles are an optional extra—make shimmer-free dough in vibrant colours to start a collection.

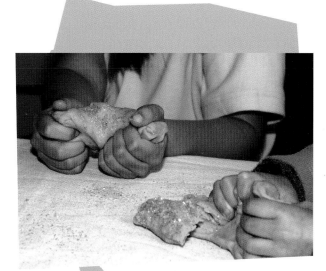

fig. 1

fig. 2

fig. 3

13

SCRATCH IT AND SEE

CINDY HOPPER

Invite your friends over and make your own homemade scratch art paper. It is very simple and lots of fun, so scratch it up!

● ●

MATERIALS
- White card or heavyweight copy paper
- Wax crayons
- Black tempera paint
- Paintbrushes or foam pads
- Washing up liquid
- Toothpicks
- Scissors
- Ruler
- Bowl or yoghurt pot

● ●

INSTRUCTIONS

1 Draw a rectangle in the centre of the paper or card and colour in all the space inside the rectangle with crayons, pressing down hard. The crayoned area should be waxy and slightly shiny with no white showing. Use a rainbow of colours in any way you like: make stripes, squares or just random scribbles (fig. 1).

2 Cut out the rectangle. Draw straight lines with a ruler before you cut for neat edges.

3 In an old bowl or yoghurt pot, mix approx. 2 tablespoons of paint with a couple of drops (quarter teaspoon) of washing-up liquid (it helps the paint stick to the crayon). Paint the entire page with the paint (fig. 2). Leave to dry—this will take about an hour.

4 When the paper is completely dry, get scratching with a toothpick (fig. 3). Scratch as you would draw with a pencil to reveal a magical, multi-coloured masterpiece!

tips

You can use your paper to make a whole range of stationery.

Note cards
Cut a shape out of your finished paper and glue it to the front of a blank note card. Your friends and family would love to get such a special note!

Ornaments
Cut out shapes and make a hole at the top with a hole-punch. Add loops of yarn or ribbon to make Christmas tree ornaments.

Bookmarks
Cut a strip from your paper, punch a hole at the top and add a tassel of yarn.

14
ROLL WITH IT
MARBLE PAINTING

AOIFE CLIFFORD

Use your marbles to paint instead of fingers and brushes! This activity is quick to organise and is lots of fun for children aged two years and up. Once the junior Jackson Pollock has been exhibited it can be recycled as wrapping paper.

MATERIALS
- 4 plastic cups or old yoghurt pots
- 4 metal spoons
- 4 colours of poster paint
- 4 marbles or small plastic balls
- Large cardboard box with lid removed (a large shoe box will do)
- White drawing paper

INSTRUCTIONS

1 Cut paper to the same size as the bottom of the box. Prepare multiple copies for when you are on a roll!

2 Fill each cup with a different coloured paint—each should only be a quarter full in case of accidents.

3 Place the paper in the bottom of the box.

4 Put a marble in each of the cups.

5 Stir the marble around with the spoon until it is covered in paint.

6 Use the spoon to place the marble in the box.

7 Tilt the box to make the marble roll back and forth, creating patterns on the paper.

8 Repeat with as many of the colours as you want.

15

MONKEY NUT NECKLACE

RACHEL MOGFORD

Cheeky monkeys (and hip cats) will love this nutty necklace. When you've finished wearing it, hang it on a tree so the birds can enjoy it too!

MATERIALS
- Monkey nuts
- Length of string or yarn
- Big thick yarn needle

INSTRUCTIONS

1 Thread the needle with a length of wool or string, a bit longer than you want your necklace to be. Tie a knot in the end of the string to stop the monkey nuts falling off.

2 Carefully stab through the middle of each monkey nut with the needle, and thread onto the string.

3 When the string is almost full with monkey nuts, tie the ends together and hey presto—a cheap and cheerful piece of jewellery!

tip

Paint with poster paint for a colourful version (although the birds won't be able to eat this one!).

16

PECKY BEAK PUPPET

JIM MORRIS

Like his friend Mr Cylinder Head, Pecky Beak loves a good old chinwag. Get chattering with this brash beaky bird puppet.

MATERIALS

- 2 A4 (18.3×11.7 in) sheets of card (of the same or contrasting colours)
- Sellotape or Scotch tape
- 1 white sticky label
- 1 elastic band
- Marker pen or felt tip

INSTRUCTIONS

1 Carefully cut each piece of card into 6 triangles (fig. 1).

2 Lay 2 triangles flat and tape them securely together at the base so that you end up with a narrow diamond shape (fig. 2).

3 Add 4 more triangles on either side of the 2 triangles (figs. 3+4).

4 Fold and tape the triangle flaps together at either end (figs. 5+6).

5 Fold the shape around to make a beak (fig. 7)

6 Cut out 2 circles from the white sticky label, draw a big black dot in the middle and stick them on either side of the beak to make eyes.

7 Add feathers by cutting rectangles of card and making lots of straight cuts close to eachother. Stick the feathery bits to the top of the open end of the beak.

8 Cut an elastic band in half and stick one end to each side of the back of the beak with tape (fig. 8) and start chattering!

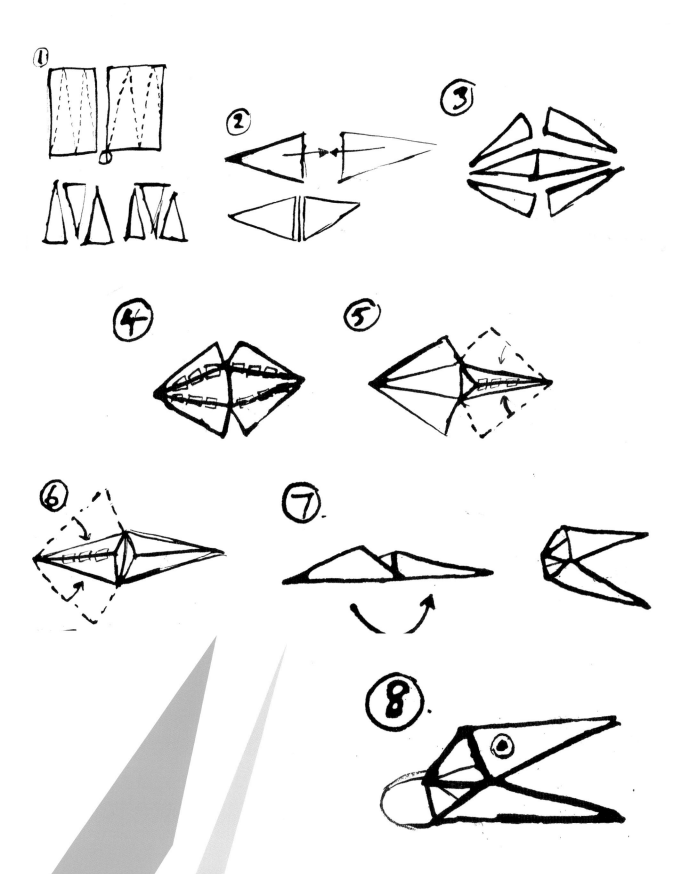

17

POTATOES FOR T!

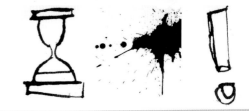

LAURA HARRIS

Why eat potatoes when you can make a neat printed t-shirt with them? Laura Harris shows how old fashioned potato printing can make a fashion statement

. . . .

MATERIALS
- Plenty of newspaper
- Thin card
- Pencil
- Child safety scissors
- Large potatoes
- Small sharp kitchen knife
- Scrap fabric
- Sponge or foam brushes
- Pale coloured t-shirt
- Water-based fabric paints such as Dylon (steer clear of oil-based paints).
- Tea towel
- Iron
- Tissues

. . . .

INSTRUCTIONS

1 Choose your design. If you want to make a flower or star, trace the shape in the template or photo (fig. 1) opposite onto a piece of thin card. Alternatively, draw out your own design. Don't make them too small or cutting the potato will be fiddly, but they must also not be bigger than the chosen potato. If you want to make the robot print, draw three different sized rectangles.

2 Cut out the shapes to use as templates and cover the table with newspaper.

3 Cut a potato in half. Dry the cut edge with a tissue, which will be a bit sticky. Use your card shape as a template to draw onto your potato and then using a small knife cut around the shape being careful not to cut into the shape and only round the outside.
You will need to cut away the outside pieces of potato, leaving the shape raised like a stamp (fig. 1).

4 If you have another shape, use the other half of the potato to make another stamp in the same way.

5 Cut a piece of sponge for each colour of paint you are using and put a small amount of each into a different saucer.

6 Use a scrap of fabric to practice printing with the potato. Dip the sponge into the paint and dab it onto the raised potato shape. Push down hard onto the fabric to leave a print. If you have opted for the robot, print the body with the biggest rectangle first, and then the head with the mid-size. Switch to a different colour paint (and a new sponge) and print arms and legs with the smallest rectangle.

7 When you have mastered the perfect potato print (not too much paint and not too little) prepare your t-shirt. Make sure your hands are paint free first! Fold up some newspaper and lay it flat inside the t-shirt in order to stop the paint soaking through to the back.

8 Decide where on the t-shirt you want to print. You can cover the other areas with newspaper to avoid dripping paint on them. Repeat step 6 until you are happy with your design. Add details like the robots eyes and aerials by dipping a pencil in paint and drawing them on. Leave to dry. Once dry, fix the paint by covering with a tea towel and ironing over the top of the print on a hot heat for 2–3 minutes.

fig. 1

TEMPLATE

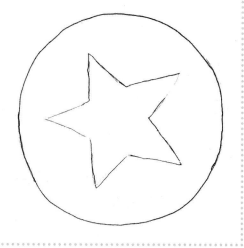

tips

Try and keep your fingers clean to avoid smudgy marks.

You can print on the back of the t-shirt, on the arm, the side — placement is half of the design!

Print on different things: a bag for school or a fabric covered lampshade to decorate your room.

CUNNING CRAFTS

CRAFTS

AGES 7+

18

COLLECTING BUTTONS

NICO AND KATIE

Collecting buttons is a special adventure—you never quite know what you might find. Here are some tips on starting a collection that can be used for all sorts of crafty projects. "There's no nicer feeling than dipping your hand in a jar of buttons and running your fingers through them," says professional button collector Nico.

MATERIALS
Buttons of all shapes and sizes, colours and materials! Here are some perfect examples:

• Sparkly glass ones (fig. 1)
• Delicate mother of pearl ones (fig. 2)
• Fun wooden ones (fig. 3)
• Some lovely old ones—I wonder who they belonged to? (fig. 4)
• Leftover glass jars

INSTRUCTIONS

1 All good button collectors have a special place to keep their sparkling treasures. Jam jars are good because they're see-through and you don't need to empty them out to see what's inside. Wash out jam jars, and other food jars when they are finished, and you'll soon have a whole shelf full of jars in which to store your collection.

2 Old buttons can be found in the strangest of places: try looking in attics, garages, down the back of the sofa, and at your grandma's house. Try asking your grandma's friends too—they never throw anything away! Jumble and car boot sales are also good places to start your search—and don't forget charity shops. Keep a look out for old tins too because sometimes buttons are shy and can be found hiding inside!

3 Don't forget to wash your buttons if they're grubby when you find them—make them sparkle!

4 When you cut up old clothes for projects (like the peg doll outfits on page 52), be sure to take the buttons off for your collection.

5 New buttons can be bought with your pocket money at big department stores and sewing shops. If you're really lucky you might find a shop that sells nothing but buttons—button heaven!

6 When your collection starts to grow, divide your buttons up into different jars according to their colour, shape, size or type. Soon you'll have so many colourful jars that your bedroom will look like a sweet shop and you'll have a button for every occasion. Don't ever be tempted to eat one though!

7 Turn over to discover an amazing button creation you can make. Buttons will also help to decorate the Bobby Dazzler Beanbag Buddy on page 102 and Knitter's Critters on page 107.

fig.1

fig.2

All photographs: Rob Hartley

fig.3

fig.4

19

CUTE AS A BUTTON NECKLACE

NICO AND KATIE

This extra special button necklace will add sparkle for a special day out or make the best ever present for your mum, auntie, sister or best friend. Threading the buttons will require a bit of patience as it is a bit fiddly, and be warned —once people see your beautiful necklace, they'll all want one. When Katie and Nico are out wearing their button jewellery they always gain a few friends along the way!

MATERIALS

- A mixture of bright buttons: the necklace shown here has 78 buttons but the number you need depends on the size of the buttons the size it needs to be to fit over your head. Pick buttons that have flat backs and buttonholes
- 5 thin shiny ribbons approx. 20–30 cm long (check clothes for ribbons in the shoulders that the shops use to stop them falling off hangers)
- Scissors
- 1 m of 'stretch magic' thread (clear is best and you can get this from craft shops)
- Multi-purpose glue

INSTRUCTIONS

1 Pick the most special button you have and thread onto the stretch magic. Poke the stretch magic through 1 buttonhole from the back of the button to the front. Pull button along so that it positioned halfway along the thread and then thread the end through the other buttonhole from front to back.

2 Add another button in the same way: push the thread through the first buttonhole from the back to the front of the button and bring the second button up to the first. Pull the thread back through the other buttonhole. Pull gently and the buttons will line up back to back.

3 Remember that the thread should always sit at the back of the button, and keep adding buttons as in step 2. As you thread on the buttons, push them together along the stretch magic so they are nice and tight. The buttons will naturally begin to overlap—you don't need to worry about positioning them, as they will decide where to sit themselves (fig. 1).

4 Thread the buttons onto both sides of the thread so that the first extra-special button will sit in the centre of your necklace.

5 Once you are happy with the length, make sure it is long enough to stretch over your head and then take both ends and loop them round to make a knot. Do this twice to make a strong double knot, and pull it as tight as you can. Trim the stretch magic so there is about 1 cm at each side of the knot.

6 Neatly cut your ribbons to 20–30 cm long. Cut the ends diagonally so they don't fray.

7 You need a helping hand with this bit: ask someone to hold the necklace with one hand on the button either side of the knot, and pull gently. Squeeze a little blob of glue onto the knot (to ensure it never comes undone) and double knot the group of ribbons over the knot and glue. Leave the glue to dry before you try!

tip

Why not make a matching bangle?

Fig. 1

20

DIGITAL KNITTING

VICTORIA WOODCOCK

Is the tricky business of perfecting the knit stitch is getting you all knotted up? Perhaps it's time to ditch the sticks and let your hands do the talking. Believe it or not, your own fingers are the perfect tools to fashion up a quick string of knit stitches that will work as a stylish skinny scarf that is, quite literally, handmade!

• •

MATERIALS
• Two spare hands!
• Any kind of thick yarn—or if what you have to hand (no pun intended this time!) is a bit on the thin side, use a few strands together.

• •

INSTRUCTIONS

Four Finger Cast On

Right-handed folk will cast onto their left hand, whilst lefties should opt for their right.

1 Position the tail of your yarn between you thumb and index finger so that it falls at the back of your hand. Grip finger and thumb together to hold the yarn in place (fig. 1).

2 Bring the yarn across the front of your index finger, behind your middle finger and across your ring finger (fig. 2).

3 Wrap the yarn around your little finger and work back toward your thumb going behind your ring finger, across the front of your middle finger and behind your index finger (fig. 3).

4 You will now have a loop around each finger (fig. 4).

5 Make another row of loops by repeating steps 2 and 3. Keep the wraps nice and loose as you don't want to cut off your circulation and this will make the knitting easier (fig. 5).

Finger Knitting

1 Hold the yarn attached to the ball between thumb and finger with the yarn coming down into your palm. This will free up your other hand to knit (fig. 6).

2 Starting at your little finger, lift the bottom loop over the top loop and over the tip of your finger. Let it go at the back of your hand (fig. 7).

3 Repeat step two on your ring, middle and index finger (fig. 8). On this first row when you get to the index finger you will be pulling the yarn tail to the back.

4 Now you will have just one loop around each finger again. Push them down toward your palm and make another row of loops above them as you did in step 5 of the Cast On (fig. 9).

5 Again lift the lower loops over the new ones and over the tips of your fingers in the same way as in steps 1 to 3. Keep making a row of new loops and lifting the lower ones over them: soon a knit creation will be growing at the back of your hand! Give the tail a tug to see the string take shape.

Free your fingers!

1 To cast off the stitches, stop when you have just one row of loops on your fingers. Lift the loop on your pinkie onto your ring finger (fig. 10).

2 Lift the lower loop on your ring finger over the upper loop and over the tip of your finger (fig. 11). In the same way, lift the loop on your ringer finger onto your middle finger and so on until you have just one stitch on your index finger.

3 Cut the yarn with a 10cm tail and thread it through this last loop to secure (fig. 12).

Attach a pompom at each end (see page 28) and wrap around your neck!

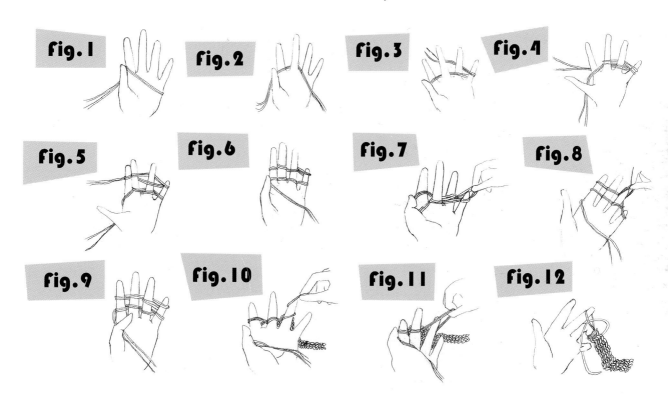

21

KNITSTER POUCH

VICTORIA WOODCOCK & CLAIRE MONTGOMERIE

This pouch can be easily fashioned by rookie knitters to stash your cash or crafty bits and bobs.

MATERIALS

- Ball of yarn worsted weight yarn, or similar, and corresponding needles
- Small amount contrasting coloured yarn
- Yarn needle
- Length of wide thick ribbon or fabric to make a strip
- Needles and thread
- Popper
- Button

INSTRUCTIONS

1 Follow the instructions on learning to knit (page 16) and cast on 20 stitches. Knit until you have a rectangle about 28 cm long (fig. 1).

2 To form the purse fold over about 10 cm and pin (fig. 2).

3 Thread the contrasting coloured yarn into the yarn needle. Starting at one of the folded corners work a blanket stitch around the edge. Start by securing the yarn to the corner with a couple of stitches through both layers. About 1 cm away from this first stitch and 1 cm in from the edge, bring the needle up through both layers. Pull the yarn through until there is a loop of yarn showing between the first and second stitch. Thread the needle through this loop and pull tight (see page 34 for blanket stitch).

4 Work blanket stitch as in step 3 all the way around the purse. It will join the two sides together and make a neat edge for the flap.

5 Pin a strip of ribbon along the inside edge of the flap. Tuck in the rough edges at either side, and pin in place. Work all the way around the edge in an overhand stitch (see pages 26+33).

6 Fold the flap down and mark where the ribbon hits the body of the purse. Sew a strip of ribbon here as in step 5. Be careful to only sew through one layer of the knit or you will sew the purse shut!

7 Sew one half of the popper to the ribbon strip on the flap. Again, fold down the flap and mark where the popper hits the ribbon. Sew the other half of the popper here.

8 Finish by sewing a button onto the front of the flap, on top of the popper.

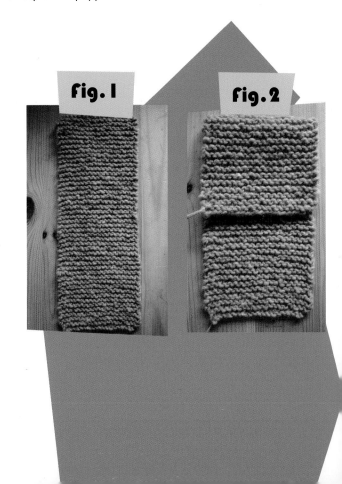

fig. 1   fig. 2

22

PLASTIC FANTASTIC PLAY MAT

VICTORIA WOODCOCK

Linoleum may be out of favour as a floor covering—all the more reason to rip it up and use it to make a play mat for cars and Lego. Not only will it spare wooden floors from scratches, it looks good enough to be a permanent feature of a room. (To turn your landscape into a village see page 126, and to craft cars for the gaffer tape highways see page 120.)

MATERIALS
- Left over linoleum off-cut
- Gaffer tape in various colours (black, silver and yellow used here)
- All-purpose strong glue
- Felt in various colours—or make your own felt from old jumpers (see page 25)
- Odd bits of carpet tiles or door mats
- Sequins or any other oddments to decorate
- Big old scissors or Stanley knife
- Sandpaper
- Spatula or old lollypop stick

INSTRUCTIONS:

1 Cut a piece of linoleum. It can be any size and shape. A wiggly, irregular shape adds interest. If you are using scissors to do this they should be old ones, as cutting through the lino will blunt them. If you have a Stanley knife, be very careful and cut on top a garage floor, grass, or another piece of lino—anything that it doesn't matter if you scratch.

2 The edges of the lino will now be quite sharp, so spend some time sanding the edge smooth so that it won't graze little knees.

3 Plan out where the roads will go—you can draw pencil lines as a guide and stick gaffer tape on top. Use your hand to smooth out the tape and ensure it is well stuck down. To make curved corners, join up two square ends first (fig. 1), then cut a small curved piece of tape to fill the gap (fig. 2). It will look like this (fig. 3).

4 You may find that some stubborn bits of tape refuse to stick, especially on the corners. Use a spatula to glue down any stray bit of tape.

5 Add road markings by cutting rectangles of tape and sticking down. Whilst doing this your scissors may get sticky and refuse to cut. If so, you will have to give them a scrub and dry them thoroughly before continuing.

6 Cut out shapes of felt (if you are using felted jumpers you will need to give them a good iron first) and carpet tiles that could be fields, car parks, lakes, etc.. Position them on the mat and draw around them lightly in pencil. Cover the lino inside the pencil lines with glue and stick down the shape. Always put the glue on the lino rather than the felt, as it would seep through the fabric otherwise.

7 Add any embellishments, like random sequins, felt flowers, or coloured circles of gaffer tape. To keep the mat in tip-top condition, keep it flat: if it is rolled or folded up the gaffer tape will come away from the lino.

tips

Why not make up your own project to try and make bridges out of old cereal boxes?

Your mat can be as fantastical as you like! Use your imagination to create an alien space station or a prehistoric landscape.

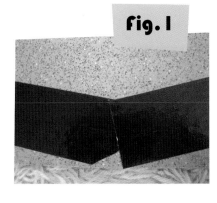

Fig. 1

Fig. 2

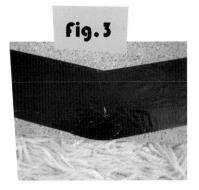

Fig. 3

23

FANCY FLORAL GIFT TAGS

LAURA FAIRBROTHER

Score present-giving points by adding a fancy floral tag to a special gift. Swap the floral theme for robots, boats or cars to impress the boys in your life. Too good to give away? Make one for your travelling bag.

MATERIALS
- Thin white card
- Pretty patterned paper
- Cotton thread in a contrasting colour to the patterned paper
- Small beads to match the cotton
- Thin ribbon
- Thin needle
- Hole punch
- Scissors or craft knife
- Glue or double-sided tape

INSTRUCTIONS

1 Copy and cut out the pattern pieces. Cut two tag shapes from the white card and one flower shape from the patterned paper. Glue the flower to one of the tags.

2 Use a needle to poke holes around the flower. It works best if you don't follow the outline of the flower precisely and make some holes that go through the card only, and others that pierce the coloured paper as well. Make six holes in a cluster in the centre and some more in lines running out from the centre. (fig. 1).

3 Thread the contrasting thread through the needle and tie a knot at the other end. Bring the needle through a hole from the back to the front of the card. Pull until the knot touches the card. Thread the needle through the next hole from the front to the back. Continue working through every hole in this way. To make a continuous line of stitches sew around the flower again making stitches in the gaps. Sew along the lines of holes inside the flower too (fig. 2).

4 Sew three beads in the centre of the flower by bringing the needle to the front of the card through one of the six holes. Thread on a bead and then bring the needle to the back again through a different hole. Repeat for the other two beads(fig. 3).

5 Using glue or double sided tape, carefully line up and attach the second tag to the back of the first, covering up the back side of the stitching.

6 Punch a hole through the tag and loop a colourful ribbon through it.

fig. 1

fig. 2

fig. 3

TEMPLATES

×2

×1

HIPPY DIPPY

VICTORIA WOODCOCK

Dip dying is as easy as it sounds and produces a striking two-tone effect.

. . . .

MATERIALS

- White t-shirt
  (or skirt, pyjama trousers, pillowcase, etc.)
- 1 or 2 packets of fabric dye
  (Dylon Cold Water Dye is sold in many high street shops and is available in a wide range of colours—if you buy this brand you also need to buy the Dylon Cold Dye Fix and some salt)
- A stick is useful for stirring the dye mixture
- Bucket or plastic box to dye the t-shirt in
- Rubber gloves to keep your mitts their normal colour!
- Clothes pegs

. . . .

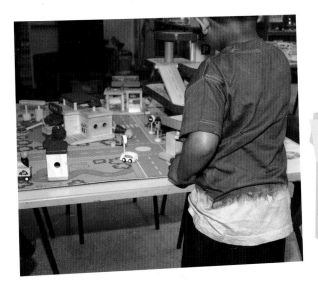

INSTRUCTIONS

1 You can either dip part of the t-shirt and leave the rest white, or dye the white part a different colour in a second stage. If using two colours, start with the darker of the two.

2 Mix up the dye and water, as per the instructions, in your chosen vessel. Keep the t-shirt out of the way when you do this, in order to avoid getting any splashes on it.

3 Carefully dip a dry t-shirt part way into the dye mixture. Even if the dye instructions tell you to use wet fabric, dipping a dry t-shirt will stop the dye bleeding, resulting in a neat, clean line. Submerge the fabric so that the dye reaches a horizontal line across the t-shirt.

4 Peg the shirt to the side of the bucket to hold it in position while it soaks. Follow the dye instructions to see how long you should leave the shirt in the dye.

5 Rinse and dry.

6 If you want to dye the remainder of the shirt, repeat steps 2–5 with the lighter shade, dipping up to the first dyed section.

tip

To make your dye go further you can dip and tie dye (see page 94) at the same time!

25
SHAKE YOUR POMPOMS SCARF

TONI CHILD

Got a thing for making pompoms? Keep hands ultra-busy and your neck toasty with a pompom scarf—a veritable wearable piece of art! Use up any yarn ods and ends you've got lying around by knotting all the pieces together.

· ·

MATERIALS

- Approx. 4–5 balls of yarn depending on desired length
- Cardboard
- Pencil
- Scissors
- Nylon thread (optional)
- Big thick needle
- Compass

· ·

INSTRUCTIONS

1 Make multiple pompoms following the instructions on page 28. You will need approx. 20, depending on the size of the pompoms and the size of the neck it will be wrapped around. Making 20 pompoms is hard work! Make a couple every time you feel like it, and eventually you will have enough.

2 Lay your pompoms out in a line, organising the composition of the scarf in terms of size and colour. Cut a piece of nylon thread, or a length of yarn, that is 20 cm longer than the pompom line.

3 Thread the needle with yarn or nylon thread and tie numerous knots at the other end to make one big knot. Push the needle through the centre of each pompom to create a chain. Push the pompoms together so that you can't see any thread in between, but not so that they are squashed. Tie another big knot at the end and cut the yarn 2–3 cm from the knot.

STRANGE FRUIT

VICTORIA WOODCOCK

Use bright coloured paint to turn papier-mâché shapes into tasty-looking fruit. Make a tomato, apple, melon, or even a pineapple. Vegetables are also possible, of course! Alternatively, let your imagination run wild and invent your own strange fruits with bright spots and stripes!

MATERIALS
- Newspapers
- Balloons
- Wallpaper paste
  (or make you own papier-mâché paste with flour, etc., as explained on page 26)
- An assortment of plastic pots or glass jars
- Poster or acrylic paint in an assortment of colours
- Small piece of green (or whatever colour you like) card
- Scissors
- Medium sized paintbrush
- Pin

INSTRUCTIONS

1 Papier-mâché around a balloon as explained on page 26. Instead of using a solid item, blow up a balloon to the size you want your piece of fruit to be. The larger you blow the balloon, the larger the fruit! Cover all the way around the fruit, leaving just a small gap where the balloon is tied (fig. 1).

2 When you have completed three layers of paper and paste, and it is completely dry, use a pin to make a hole in the balloon near to where it is tied. Pull the balloon out of the small hole in the papier-mâché.

3 Paint the shape all over: balance it on a glass jar and paint as much of the shape as you can. Leave to dry, and then flip it over to paint the remainder (fig. 2).

4 Make a stalk by rolling up a strip of card—then gently push it into the hole in the papier-mâché fruit. Cut out leaves with a tab at one end (fig. 3). Position the tab next to the stalk.

tips

Using plain white paper for the third papier-mâché layer will help the painting process, as the newspaper print will not show through.

You can make anything you like with your shape: sit your shapes in pots and paint on faces. Add wool for hair, eyebrows and moustaches!

fig. 1

fig. 2

fig. 3

27

FRENCH FANCY

Oooh la la! French knitting produces a delicate knit tube without using any knitting needles. It does however, take two to French Knit—you need to get yourself a knitting dolly (fig. 1). They can be widely found in yarn stores and toyshops. Better still, you can make one yourself from a cotton reel and some drawing pins.

MATERIALS
• An old cotton reel
• Yarn
• 4 drawing pins
• Needle

INSTRUCTIONS

To make your very own French knitting machine, take an old wooden cotton reel and stick four drawing pins evenly around the hole in the middle (fig. 2).

Le Cast On

1 Thread the yarn through the reel: from the top where the pins are and out at the other end (fig. 3).

2 Keeping hold of the string at the bottom, wrap the yarn at the top anticlockwise around one of the pins. Bring the yarn over to the left hand side of the next pin clockwise (fig. 4).

3 Wrap the yarn anticlockwise around the next pin and repeat until each pin has a loop around it (fig. 5).

You Tube

By hooking loops off the pins and into the centre of the reel a knitted tube will miraculously appear.
1 Continuing to work clockwise around the reel, pull the yarn across the front of the first pin above the original loop. Insert your needle into the original loop (fig. 6).

2 Lift the loop over the yarn and the top of the pin. Let go of the loop. The yarn pulled across the pin will now have formed a loop. There should be one loop on each pin at all times (fig. 7).

3 Repeat steps 1 and 2 on the next pin clockwise. Work round and round the reel in this manner. After every few stitches pull the yarn tail at the bottom of the reel to encourage the knit tube to move through the reel (fig. 8).

Le Cast Off

1 When your tube is the desired length stop passing the yarn over the pins. Lift a loop with the needle (fig. 9).

2 Lift the loop onto the next pin along clockwise (fig. 10).

3 Insert the needle into the bottom loop on the pin and lift it over the other loop and the top of the pin. Let go of the loop (fig. 11).

4 With the loop left on the pin repeat steps 1 to 3. Continue until there is just one loop left. Cut the yarn with a 10cm or so tail, lift the last loop off the pin and thread the tail through the loop to secure.

tips

French knitting makes great arms and legs for knit monsters (fig. 12)!

With a longer tube (about a metre) you can make the pom-pom string on the next page.

POMPOM STRING-A-LONG

VICTORIA WOODCOCK & CLAIRE MONTGOMERIE

Made a long French-knit tube? Don't know what to do with it? How about adding some pompoms for an eye-catching window adornment? After all, they have been seen in fashionable London homes and lovely knit boutique Loop...

MATERIALS
- French knitting dolly or cotton reel and four drawing pins.
- Needle or crochet hook
- LOTS of brightly coloured yarn—ask a knitter for their leftovers!
- Pompom maker with variety of sizes, or see page 28 to make your own

tip

If French knitting is just too time consuming, use a thick piece of elastic to string up your pompoms. Warning: cats will love playing with this!

INSTRUCTIONS

1 French knit a tube (see previous page) a metre or so long, or the length of the window where you intend to hang the pompom string.

2 Follow the instructions on your pompom maker and wrap yarn around both halves of the device. Lock the two halves together and now string the tube through the centre hole. Position the pompom maker at the point along the tube where you want the pompom to be. If you have constructed your own pompom maker from cardboard, warp the yarn around as explained on page 28.

3 Again, following the instructions on your specific pompom maker, cut through the wrapped yarn and pull a string tightly around the middle. When you remove the pompom maker it should hold tight to the tube. If it is a bit loose use a needle and thread to sew a few stitches through the centre of the pompom and the tube.

4 Repeat using different coloured yarns and different sized pompom makers. To make a speckled pompom, wrap two different coloured strands of yarn together. For the bottom pompom make it separately from the tube, and then tie together the yarn tail on the tube and the remaining yarn from around the pompom to attach.

SHAKE YOUR MARACAS

VICTORIA WOODCOCK

Make some noise with papier-mâché. A maraca can be made in the same way as the papier-mâché fruit on page 82—just add some tuneful beans and a handle to shake it!

MATERIALS

- Newspapers
- Balloons
- Wallpaper paste (or make you own paste with flour, etc. as explained on page 26)
- An assortment of plastic pots or glass jars
- Poster or acrylic paint in an assortment of colours
- Scissors
- Medium sized paintbrush
- Sturdy wooden stick approx. 25–30 cm long (buy it from the hardware store and get them to cut it for you)
- Dried beans
- PVA glue (optional)
- Assortment of ribbons and fabric scraps (optional)
- Drawing pin (optional)

INSTRUCTIONS

1 Papier-mâché around a balloon as explained on page 26. Instead of using a solid item, blow up a balloon to the size you want the maraca to be. Don't fully blow up the balloon, or your maraca will be to heavy to carry, let alone shake! Completely cover the balloon in paper and paste, leaving just a small gap where the balloon is tied. This is where the handle will go.

2 When you have completed three layers of paper and paste (remembering to leave to dry between layers), and it is completely dry, use a pin to make a hole in the balloon near to where it is tied. Pull the balloon out of the small hole in the papier-mâché.

3 Paint the shape all over: place it in a glass jar, and paint as much of the shape as you can. Leave to dry, then flip it over and paint the remainder.

4 Paint on a pattern—try spots or stripes. You could also paint on your name. Leave to dry.

5 Make a couple of small snips with scissors around the hole in the papier-mâché and drop some beans into the shape. Push the stick into the hole until the end touches the inside of the shape. It should hold tight, but you can also add a dab of glue to secure.

6 Your maraca is now complete, but you might also want to paint the handle. To add a tail cut pieces of ribbon and strips of fabric approx. 30–40 cm in length. Push the drawing pin through the centre points of the strips and stick it into the end of the handle.

30

HOME IS WHERE THE HEART IS DOORMAT

CINDY HOPPER

Leave your mark on a doormat, and I don't mean a footprint! No, dress up your front door with a designer hand-printed doormat. Make your own stamps that will offer a seasonal greeting to all visitors.

MATERIALS

- Carpet samples in a regular pile (not shag pile or textured carpet)—ask at a carpet store, they may even give them to you for free! Ask for one extra carpet sample to practice on
- Acrylic paint
- Thin, dense foam craft sheets (like a yoga mat)
- Scraps of wood—ask at a timber yard or hardware shop if you don't know anyone who would have some lying around their garage
- Rubber cement or other strong glue
- Foam paint brush

INSTRUCTIONS

1 Make templates in paper for the stamps. You can copy the heart shape here or make your own. Draw around each template twice on the foam, because each stamp needs two layers of foam. Cut out the shapes.

2 Stick the shapes onto a block of wood using rubber cement, or other strong glue. Use a foam paintbrush to apply the cement or glue and attach one layer of foam at a time (fig. 1). Once you have glued on both layers of foam, put something heavy and flat (like a big book or two) on top of the stamp while the glue dries, to stop the foam from curling. Leave to dry for 20–30 minutes. Repeat for each stamp you're making (fig. 2).

3 Use a foam brush to cover the foam shape on a stamp with acrylic paint (this is not entirely washable, so be careful). This is easier than dipping and keeps the area around the stamp clean, which is very important. Use a lot of paint.

4 Practice printing on the extra carpet sample. Press the stamp into the carpet and rock and jiggle the stamp to work the paint into the carpet. Practice until you get the feel of the amount of paint, pressure and jiggling you need to apply! (fig. 3). If you find it hard to apply enough pressure, get someone to lend you a hand. If your print comes off light, simply take your foam brush and work a bit more paint in those areas.

5 Print with all stamps and various coloured paints on the final carpet sample. To print with a smaller stamp inside a larger print make sure the paint has dried first (fig. 4).

6 Once you are finished, the stamps can be rinsed off with water. Allow them to dry completely before storing.

tips

If you don't want to make your own stamps you can always use the large foam die-cut sponges found at craft stores. Make sure to dampen your sponge before dipping it into the paint.

The stamps can be used on paper and card too. You won't need to use as much paint or jiggle the stamp when printing on a smooth surface, just press straight down.

TEMPLATE

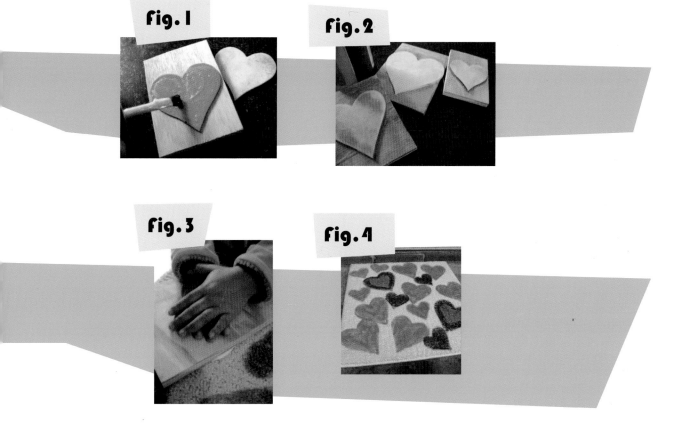

fig. 1

fig. 2

fig. 3

fig. 4

31

PILLOWCASE PIRATE

LAURA SPRING

Pieces of eight and a parrot are optional extras for this swashbuckling pirate outfit that is ingeniously constructed from two pillowcases. What's more, there is virtually no sewing required. Shiver me timbers! It's so simple you can use the idea as a starting point for your own costume creations.

MATERIALS
- 2 plain white pillowcases
- 2.5 cm wide masking tape
- Black fabric paint
- Paintbrush
- Some carrier bags (the thicker, flatter ones are best)
- 50 cm black felt
- 50 cm thin black elastic
- Fabric glue
- A few beads or plastic jewels (optional)
- Pencil
- Ruler
- A4 piece of paper
- Sharp scissors
- Pins
- Approx. 1.5 m length of plain scrap fabric
- Needle and thread

INSTRUCTIONS

1 Fold a pillowcase in half lengthways to find the centre point of the short folded edge (the edge that is stitched closed). Make a small cut into the fabric at this point and cut along the seam in both directions for 11 cm. It may help to measure and mark the points before you cut. You will end up with a slit along measuring 22 cm—your head will go through here!

2 Make two armholes along the two long edges. Start at the corners either side of the head hole and cut along the seam for 17 cm (fig. 1).

3 Lay the pillowcase out in front of you so that the head hole is furthest away. With a pencil and ruler, mark out the stripes. Starting at one corner next to the head hole, measure 2.5 cm along the long length and make a small mark. Repeat the measurement on the opposite side. Stick masking tape horizontally across the pillowcase lining up the top of the edge of the tape with the pencil marks. Flip the pillowcase over so that the tape makes a loop around the case.

4 Measure 2.5 cm down from the bottom edge of the tape on both sides and position a strip of masking tape as in step 3. Repeat until there are horizontal loops of tape evenly spaced around the whole pillowcase (fig. 2).

5 On a flat surface with plenty of room, put the plastic bags inside the pillowcase and paint the strips of fabric that are exposed with the fabric paint. Leave to dry, and then turn over to paint the other side. Leave to dry fully and fix according to the paint instructions—this will usually involve ironing the fabric.

6 Finally, cut triangles of different shapes and sizes into the bottom edge for a jagged finish.

7 Enlarge and photocopy the skull and crossbones template onto a piece of paper and cut out. Pin the pieces to the black felt and cut around the shapes. Sew or glue a couple of plastic jewels or beads on for the eyes, and stick the felt to the centre front of the pillowcase with fabric glue.

8 To make the eye patch, enlarge and photocopy the template onto paper and cut out. Pin the paper shape to the felt and cut out twice. Glue the two pieces together. When dry, hold the patch to your eye and measure the amount of elastic you need by pulling it around your head. Make sure the elastic has enough tension, but isn't going to be so tight it will hurt! Sew the two ends to either side of the patch and decorate as desired with beads.

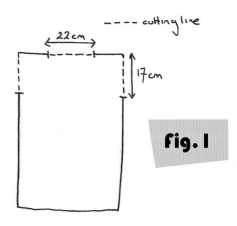

fig. 1

9 To make the bandana, cut up both the long side seams of the other pillowcase and open it out flat. As in step 7, cut out felt crossbones (probably about four will work well) and glue to the fabric at the centre of one of the long lengths. Leave to dry. To wear, place the centre of the fabric on your head and tie securely in a knot at the base of the neck. If there is too much spare fabric, remove and cut equal amounts from each end.

10 To make the belt, roughly chop into the scrap of fabric to create a worn, jaggy edge. Tie it loosely round the waist—if it is a bit long, just chop a bit off.

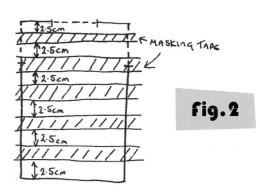

fig. 2

TEMPLATES

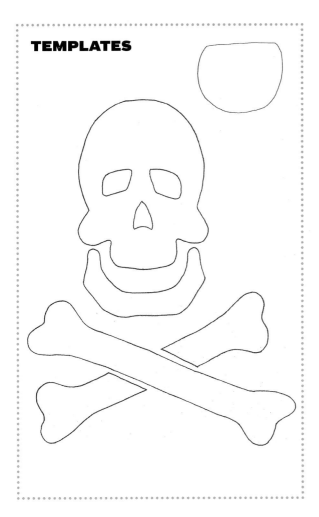

32

PILLOWCASE PRINCE OF THIEVES

LAURA SPRING

Dress to impress as the infamous outlaw of Sherwood Forest, Robin Hood. Laura Spring demonstrates another fancy dress option that can be crafted from a pillowcase. With more sewing skills needed than for the pirate outfit, it's bound to be pillowcases at dawn!

MATERIALS

- 1 green pillowcase
- 50 cm green felt
- Matching green thread
- 150×12 cm of contrasting fabric (patterned or plain)
- 30 cm thin black elastic
- 4 buttons
- Sharp scissors
- Sewing machine (optional)
- Embroidery thread or wool in a contrasting colour
- A yarn needle (preferably one with a large eye)
- Feather
- Dressmaker's pins
- Iron
- Tape measure

INSTRUCTIONS

For the costume

1 Repeat steps 1 and 2 from the pirate instructions on the previous page with a green pillowcase.

2 Starting at the centre point in the head hole, cut a straight line through one layer of fabric towards the bottom of the pillow about 14 cm in length. Fold over the corners from the point where you began cutting back to create a collar. Make sure triangles are even and pin into place. Sew a button on each folded back triangle where the pins are (fig. 1).

3 Place the pillowcase on a flat surface and cut triangles of different shapes and sizes into the bottom edge for a jagged finish. Do the same at each armhole.

For the belt

4 Lay the piece of 150×12 cm fabric out on a flat surface with the right side facing up towards you. Fold it in half lengthways and pin along the edges to hold in position —this will make a long thin tube.

5 Sew a straight line approx. 1 cm in from the edge of the fabric along the long edge and one of the smaller edges—use a sewing machine or sew by hand with a running stitch (see page 32).

6 Chop off the corner where the 2 stitching lines cross (fig. 2) and turn inside out—a little patience is required here as it's a bit fiddly! Once it's the right way out, tuck the rough edges into the open end and hand stitch it closed with an overhand stitch (see pages 26 and 33). Press flat with a hot iron.

For the hat

7 Cut out four 21×31 cm rectangles of green felt. Place two rectangles together and sew in along all edges roughly 1 cm from the edge of the fabric—use a running stitch or select a medium size straight stitch on your machine. Repeat this with the other two rectangles. The rectangles of double thickness will make the hat stiffer and stop it from flopping.

8 Pin the two thick rectangles on top of each other. With the contrasting thread, sew a blanket stitch (see page 34) along one short and one long side.

Fig. I

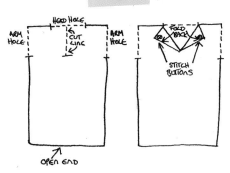

Fig. 2

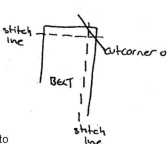

Fig. 3

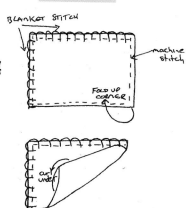

9 Curl back the two free corners (fig. 3) and pin into place. With matching thread, make a few small discreet stitches to secure both folds. To finish, slide the stem of the feather into one of the curls and hand stitch into place by going through the fabric and around the feather stem several times.

For the boots

10 Measure the distance between your anklebone and knee and add on 15 cm (A). Also measure around your leg just under the knee (B). Cut two rectangles of green felt in these dimensions—A×B.

11 Fold over one of the shorter edges by 15 cm and pin. Cut triangles into the edges that are folded over for a jagged edge.

Fig. 4

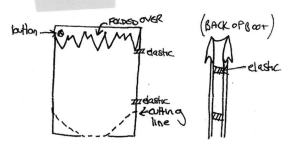

12 At the opposite short edge, cut out a shape as shown in fig. 4. Sew a couple of pieces of elastic (approx. 5 cm long) on as marked. Sew the other end of the elastic onto the other side of the felt in the same place. You can alter the length of the elastic if it is either too baggy or tight, but it shouldn't be if you've measured around the leg correctly. Sew a button onto the folded over bit of felt.

13 Repeat steps 11 and 12 with the remaining rectangle for your other leg. Make sure you sew the button on the opposite side to the first one, so that they are both facing out to the side when worn.

33
T-SHIRT TIE DYE FOR

VICTORIA WOODCOCK

Tie dye: hip or hippy? Who cares! Tie dying gives a dull white t-shirt a make over and, more importantly, is a fun way to spend an afternoon. In the 60s and 70s this easy (peasy!—see below to get the pun!) technique was all the rage. Tie your t-shirt up in knots to get the Summer of Love vibe.

MATERIALS

- Old white t-shirt
  (or any other fabric item—cotton ones work best)
- Lots of elastic bands. The thicker the bands the thicker the white rings of your circles will be
- Dried peas or other small hard round objects such as marbles
- Packet of fabric dye (Dylon Cold Water Dye is sold in many high street shops and is available in a wide range of colours—if you buy this brand you also need to buy the Dylon Cold Dye Fix and some salt)
- A stick—useful for stirring the dye mixture
- Bucket or plastic box to dye t-shirt in
- Rubber gloves to keep your mitts their normal colour!

INSTRUCTIONS

1 Lay your t-shirt flat on a table with the peas and elastic bands to one side. Start by holding a dried pea inside the t-shirt—this will be the centre of your circular design, the middle of the shirt is a good place to start (fig. 1).

2 Gather the fabric around the pea and hold in place with finger and thumb (fig. 2).

3 Take an elastic band and wrap it around fabric where your fingers are. The pea is now trapped in the fabric and this will create the first white circle of your design. Secure the elastic band tightly—this is important as it prevents the dye getting to the part of the t-shirt underneath (fig. 3).

4 To add another layer to the circle, wind a second elastic band around the fabric—leaving a space between the two (fig. 4).

5 You can add as many bands as you like after the pea. The more bands you place after one pea the more rings the circle will have. You can create different effects by changing the distance between the bands.

6 To add another circle add another pea in another space and follow steps 1–5.

7 Keep adding peas and elastic bands until there is no space to add any more—or when you think your design is complete! Your t-shirt will now look like a strange sea creature!

8 Now dye the t-shirt according to the instructions on the packet. You might want to do this outside —otherwise make sure you mix up the dye on a covered surface.

9 Unravel the bands to reveal your design.

tip

Make a design with just one big circle on the front by positioning just one pea and placing elastic bands around it until you reach the edges of the t-shirt.

fig. 1

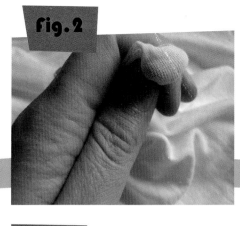

fig. 2

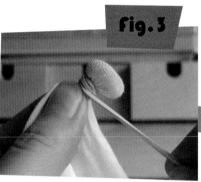

fig. 3

fig. 4

34

COLOUR BY STITCHES T-SHIRT

SUZIE FRY

Show off childhood creativity by transferring a drawing on to a plain t-shirt. Forget fancy printing in favour of simple embroidery that can be mastered by all skill levels and is quick and easy to complete with a minimum of purchases and tools. The project works for children of all ages: adults can stitch up drawings for very young children (who will be fascinated to see their doodle transformed), whilst older children will be able to complete the whole project on their own. If you can bear to part with your creation, they are bound to be a hit as presents for parents, grandparents and friends.

MATERIALS
- Plain white cotton t-shirt—one without too much stretch
- Drawing paper and felt-tip pens
- Pencil or water-soluble fabric marker
- Embroidery threads and needle
- Embroidery hoop
  (optional, but it makes the job easier)

INSTRUCTIONS

1 Draw a picture—any picture—on plain white paper in deep-coloured felt-tips (as they are easier to see through fabric later).

2 Place the picture inside the t-shirt and position it in your desired location (the top left front will result in the finished picture being over the heart). In good light you should be able to see the outline of the drawing. If not, simply retrace the picture in a stronger colour.

3 Trace the drawing through the t-shirt using a lead pencil or water-soluble marker. At this stage you may want to simplify the picture as strong images with a minimum of lines and solid blocks will be easiest to embroider later. However, bear in mind that the picture shouldn't be 'perfect'; if you neaten it up too much it will no longer look like it was drawn by a child.

4 If you are using an embroidery hoop, separate the two sections and place the non-adjustable hoop inside the t-shirt, underneath the drawing (or part of the drawing if the design is bigger than the hoop). Place the adjustable hoop on top, but don't pull the fabric too tight as you will distort the image and stretch the t-shirt out of shape. Once the fabric is evenly stretched across the hoop, tighten the screw.

5 Start the embroidery by sewing along the solid outlines using a basic running or backstitch (see page 32). Keep the stitches small and not too tight, as the shirt will stretch when worn and tight stitches might be broken. Backstitch is particularly good for giving some stretch and gives a nice continuous line. Keep close to the original drawing by using the same colours.

6 Next fill in any blocks of colour with rough rows of stitches. Remember that the t-shirt will stretch more across the body than from top to bottom, so it is better to work in vertical row when filling in areas. Use running stitches, as used in the red areas (fig. 1), whilst rows of chain stitch will add texture if you want a bit more of a challenge (see page 34).

7 Tie off ends neatly and wash the t-shirt to remove any traces of the drawing.

fig. 1

35
PHOTOGRAPHIC FLOWER POWER

LOGLIKE

Merge photography and craft to make sculptural slot-together flowers that stay bright all year long. Gain some extra nature knowledge along the way by learning the names of the plants and wildlife you photograph for your artwork.

• •

MATERIALS
- A digital camera (preferably with a 'macro' or close-up option)
- A dry day!
- Some outdoor plants, flowers and insects to photograph
- Thin card (a cereal packet works well)
- PVA glue
- Scissors
- A pencil or pen
- Tracing paper
- A container to use as a vase
- 'Coated' inkjet printing paper (matte or gloss) if printing your own photos
- Small pebbles or sand
- Telephone directory or heavy book

• •

INSTRUCTIONS

1 Have fun outdoors looking for plants and flowers with bright colours and interesting shapes. Also try to find cute and creepy insects, slugs and snails. Photograph what you find. Take close-ups if you have a macro setting, so what you're looking at fills the photo area. Take at least 20 photos, preferably more.

2 Print out the photographs. If you're printing them at home, try and set the print quality to 'best photo' or 'fine' and if possible turn off 'high speed printing'. If it prints out in stripes, select the 'clean the print heads' option until it stops. They don't need to be full-sized photos; if you can, try printing out nine pictures per A4 (8.3×11.7 inches).

3 Glue the photographs to either side of a thin piece of card. Make sure that you don't get glue on the front of the photos or the ink will run. Leave to dry under a telephone directory or a weighty book, to stop them from curling.

4 Trace the templates. Place the templates on the photo cards, and draw around as many times as you can.

5 Cut out the circle shapes first.

6 Now cut out the slots: snip into each slot twice, making the slots roughly as wide as the card is thick. So, if you are using very thin card, make narrow slots; thicker card needs wider slots. To remove the slim piece of excess card, grip it tightly close to the base, and twist —it should come away without tearing the image.

7 Choose your vase. Carefully fill the bottom with something heavy like sand or pebbles to stop it toppling over.

8 Start off your flower sculpture by widening a slot in the first paper flower, so that it wedges snugly onto the vase edge. For an extra stable base, attach two pieces to the vase and wedge another into slots on both to start building your plant.

9 Build your sculpture up and out, by adding more flower circles. Make sure to line up the slots, and carefully push them all the way in.

10 Keep adding and re-arranging until you run out of flower circles or are happy with your creation. Lop-sided can be cool!

TEMPLATES

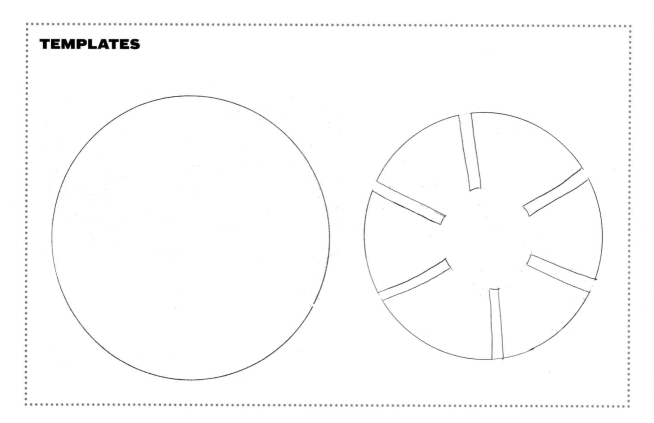

36

X-RATED DOOR SIGN

VICTORIA WOODCOCK

Cross-stitch a message to nosy brother and sisters. This project is suitable for beginners: it's simple—and to the point!

MATERIALS

- Approx. 3–4 skeins of embroidery thread in any colours
- 25×25 cm 6-count Binca cross-stich fabric —great for beginners
- Scissors
- Large blunt needle—a plastic one will do for this fabric
- Iron
- Embroidery hoop (optional)
- Frame (optional)

INSTRUCTIONS

1 Cut a length of embroidery thread approx. 30–40 cm long and thread it through the needle. Pull about 10 cm of thread through the needle and tie a couple of knots at the other end.

2 You should start at the top left hand corner with the letter K about 5 cm from the top left hand corner of the fabric. See page 15 on how to cross-stitch and follow the chart by counting the number of Xs on the design, and recreating them on the fabric. Remember that the first stitches of the X should always slope in the same direction.

3 You can use a different colour for each letter, knotting the thread when finished to secure, before cutting.

4 Iron the design gently to neaten it up.

5 You can stick your X-rated message to a bedroom or cupboard door as is, or you might want to add a frame for extra impact!

6 To frame, cut a rectangle of cardboard the same size as the glass of the frame you are using. Place the cross-stitch face down on an ironing board and place the cardboard on top of the design, making sure it runs parallel to the lines of holes in the fabric. Fold over the rough edges up to the cardboard one by one and press (Figs. 1+2). Pop the rectangle into the frame without the glass.

tips

You can get Binca from fabric shops or websites such as www.sewessential.co.uk—Google for other retailers.

Make up your own message or cross-stitch your name, using squared paper to design the letters.

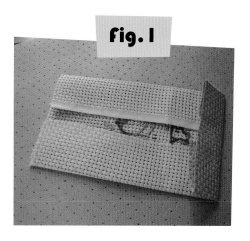

Fig. 1

Fig. 2

PATTERN

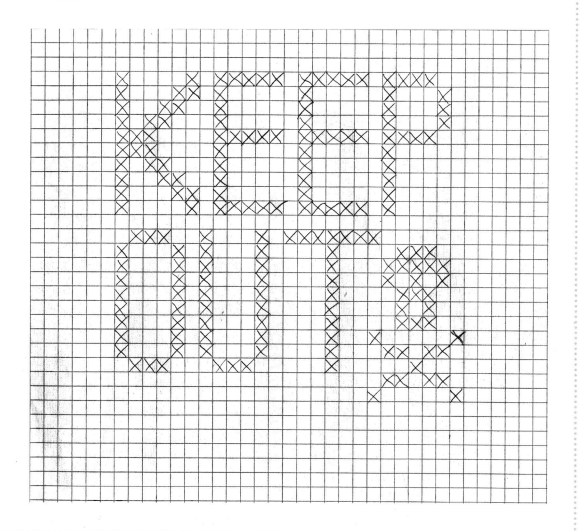

37

BOBBY DAZZLER
BEAN BAG BUDDY

ROSIE SHORT

With a minimum of sewing skills, old clothes and odd buttons you can make a friendly — if not slightly strange — little creature!

. . . .

MATERIALS
- T-shirt
- Scissors
- Pen or chalk
- Needle and thread
- Chopstick or paintbrush
- Lentils or dried beans
- Funnel
- Buttons

. . . .

INSTRUCTIONS:

1 Cut a piece of fabric approx. 25×25 cm from an old t-shirt and fold in half with the right sides together (fig. 1) — so the t-shirt fabric that faced outwards when worn is folded together.

2 Enlarge and photocopy the template. Cut out the shape and place it on the folded material. Draw around the stencil in pen or chalk if you have chosen a dark colour (fig. 2).

3 Hand-stitch along the line you've drawn through both layers of fabric, with a running or back stitch (see page 32). Keep the stitches very close together so the lentils don't come out later. You must leave a space of 3 cm unsewn on one side of the cat (fig. 3).

4 Cut round the shape, leaving a space of about 1 cm from the sewn line (fig. 4).

5 Now turn your cat inside out. This can be a bit tricky. Use a chopstick to shove all fabric through the hole then push arms and legs out with the stick too (fig. 5).

6 To stuff the doll you need to put a funnel into the hole on the side of the cat and pour in dried beans or lentils. Use the stick to push the beans to the bottom of arms and legs (fig. 6).

7 Stitch up the side hole with a whipstitch (see page 33). You might also need to stitch up any holes you might have made while turning it inside out (fig. 7).

8 Sew on buttons for eyes and make a stitch or two for a mouth (fig. 8): say hello to your new cat!

TEMPLATE

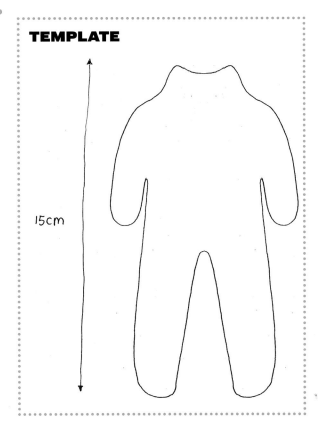

15cm

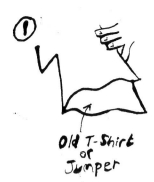

① Old T-Shirt or Jumper

②

③ LEAVE A GAP!

CUT OUT THE CAT....

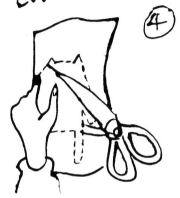

④

⑤ Stick

Poke beans with Stick....

⑥ Funnel

FILL Hole with beans & lentils....

⑦

Stitch it up!

⑧ Button

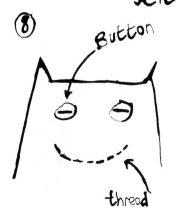

thread

38

TOTALLY TUTU

MICHELLE DUXBURY-TOWNSLEY

Quite literally fancy dress, a tutu adds instant princess points, and in red and black, will knock the spots off a shop-bought pink version. This simple tutu requires very little sewing and can be adjusted for ladybird growth!

MATERIALS
- Black and red tulle or dress netting (see instruction step 1 on how to calculate the amount of fabric you will need)
- Approx. 2 m of 7 mm red and black ribbon
- Needle and thread
- Scissors
- Tape measure
- Dressmaker's pins
- Safety pin

INSTRUCTIONS

1 Calculate the amount of fabric you need by taking a waist measurement and multiplying it by three (or even by four for extra puffiness!). Decide how long you want the tutu to be and multiply that measurement by two. For example, a 20 cm-long tutu to fit a 60 cm waist would require each piece of tulle to measure 40×180 cm. You need six pieces of tulle this size—four pieces in black and two in red. Take your measurements to the fabric shop and they will help you to buy the correct amount of fabric.

2 Cut out four pieces of black tulle and two pieces of red tulle according to your measurements.

3 Cut one piece of each ribbon about 20 cm longer than the waist edge of the tulle. Therefore, using the earlier example, you would need a 2 m piece of each coloured ribbon.

4 Layer the tulle as desired. For example, two black layers, followed by two red and the remaining black pieces.

5 Fold the tulle, with all six layers together, in half lengthways—long edge to long edge. Use a few pins to hold the fold in place.

6 Create a channel to thread the ribbon through. You can do this by hand sewing with a running stitch (see page 32) or using a sewing machine. Sew a straight line approx. 2 or 3 mm below the fold along the length of the tulle. Then sew another line approximately 1 cm below and parallel to the first line. Secure all the ends by knotting or back stitching.

7 Thread the ribbon through the channel in the tulle. The best way to do this is to attach a small safety pin through both pieces of ribbon and use it to guide the ribbon through the channel.

8 Gather the tulle along the ribbon to the desired waist length and secure by tying the ribbon with a bow
.

tips

You can decorate the tutu with glitter, sequins, fabric paint or cut a fancy edge—whatever takes your fancy!

Wear with the wonderful 'Wing It' wings (see next page) for a full on bug effect!

39
WING IT!

MICHELLE DUXBURY-TOWNSLEY

A pair of wings is the central ingredient to being a ladybird or other lovely insect! For a flight of fancy, wear with your ladybird tutu (on previous page).

MATERIALS
- 2 wire coathangers
- 1 pair of red tights
- Black gaffer tape
- Approx. 1 m of black elastic of a medium thickness, about 1 cm wide
- Approx. 1 m of black and red ribbon
- 1 square of black felt
- Fabric glue
- Pliers
- Wire cutters

INSTRUCTIONS

1 Cut the hook from both coathangers with the wire cutters. Use the pliers to shape each wire into a wing shape, joining up the two wire ends with a twist. Bring the two twists together and wrap gaffer tape around them until the two wire wings are securely fastened together (fig. 1).

2 Cut the legs off the tights and carefully stretch one over each wing. Pull tight and cut off any excess. Use more gaffer tape to secure the tights at the point in between the two frames. Be sure to catch all edges of the tights fabric underneath the tape (fig. 2).

3 Make a loop with the elastic that is big enough to stretch from the back, over the shoulder and under the arm of the person who is going to wear the wings, without being too tight. Tie a knot to secure. Make another loop exactly the same size (fig. 3).

4 Place the knots of the loops on top of the gaffer tape in between the wings. Attach the elastic to your wings by wrapping another strip of gaffer tape around the join, covering the knots of the loops (fig. 4).

5 Disguise the gaffer tape by wrapping ribbon around the join, leaving some long bits dangling (fig. 5).

6 Glue black felt spots onto your wings (fig. 6) and prepare to take off!

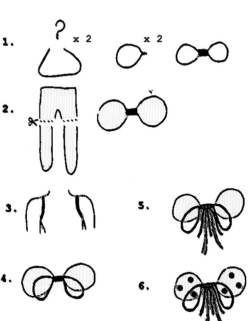

40

KNITTERS CRITTERS

VICTORIA WOODCOCK AND CLAIRE MONTGOMERIE

Aliens, monsters and all kinds of creatures can be stitched up from two knitted rectangles. All you need is a little imagination...

• •

MATERIALS

- Yarn (as specified on page 16) in at least two colours
- Needles to match the yarn (page 16)
- Yarn needle—a big plastic one is best
- Fibre fill or other stuffing
- A few dried beans—bigg-ish ones that won't pop through the knit fabric!
- Dressmakers' pins
- Buttons and scraps of fabric
- Needle and thread

• •

INSTRUCTIONS

1 Knit two rectangles as explained on pages 17–19. It doesn't matter what size your rectangles are, so long as they are roughly the same size. You can use different yarn to knit each, but try to use yarn of the same thickness with the same sized needles. To make stripes see page 22.

2 Pin the two rectangles together. Thread a 50–60 cm length of yarn through the yarn needle and sew the two layers together with a back stitch (page 24) along the two longer edges and one of the short ones. You could also quickly sew round on a sewing machine to save time.

3 Stuff your creature-to-be with stuffing and beans until it has a nice huggable feel to it. Check that the beans are big enough not to squeeze through the spaces in the knit (fig. 1).

4 Sew up the last remaining side with back stitch.

5 Add eyes, nose and mouth in any way you like. You can pin on the buttons etc first and move them around until you get the right expression! To sew on bits of fabric, pin them on and use an overhand stitch (pages 26+33) to secure (fig. 2).

tip

Messy little critters look great, so leaving yarn tails dangling, and don't worry about making your stitching too neat: it all adds to personality!

fig. 1

fig. 2

SUPER SKILLS

SKILLS AGES 11+

SKULL AND CROSS STITCH BONES

JULIE JACKSON

There was a time, not so long ago, when cross-stitching was, well, a bit dull. But this design is anything but dull—in fact it's positively glowing! This project will take time and patience, but how cool will it be to have a glowing skeleton keeping you company when you turn off the light? You'll be able to scare your friends at sleepovers when it gets dark... BOO!

● ●

MATERIALS

- Black, 14-count Aida cross-stitch material
- Skein of DMC glow-in-the-dark embroidery thread
- Size 24 embroidery or tapestry needle
- 13 or 15 cm plastic or wood embroidery hoop
- Scissors
- Handwash detergent
- Pinking shears (optional)
- Frame (optional)
- Towel
- Iron, ironing board and piece of thin cotton material

● ●

INSTRUCTIONS

1 Cut a piece of the fabric at least 30 cm wide and 40 cm tall. The actual skeleton will be about 10 cm wide and 20 cm tall, but you need a piece of material that's much larger. It's really important to have a lot of extra material around the design! Use pinking shears (the kind that make a zig-zag cut) to cut the fabric if you have them, as they prevent the material from fraying.

2 Cut a piece of embroidery thread approx. 40 cm long. Roll one end of the thread between your fingers: you'll see that what looks like one string is actually six smaller strands. Use only two strands at a time—this is very important!

You can pull two strands away from the thread and leave the other four strands for the next time you thread your needle.

3 Place the centre of the fabric in the embroidery hoop. It should be pretty taut, like the top of a drum, and will help to make the stitches even. Thread the needle and tie a knot at the other end of the thread: not a big knot, but one just big enough so that it won't pull through the material.

4 Look at the pattern overleaf and find the arrows: one at the top and one on the side. If you follow both arrows, you'll find the approximate centre of the pattern (around the skeleton's waist line). Choose one of the squares near the centre of the pattern. This square will be your first stitch. The stitch is really simple; it's just an X. Each square of the pattern is one X stitch. The special cross-stitch material is a grid of holes that maps out where the stitches go. When working with black material, it's important to have a lot of light in order to see the holes to thread the needle through.

5 In the centre of the hoop, begin stitching your chosen square by bringing the threaded needle up from the back of the fabric until the knot stops it. Use the instructions and illustrations on page 15 to see how to make a stitch. Remember to always make the first stitch of the X in the same direction (either ╱ or ╲). It doesn't matter which way, but if they're mixed, the finished piece will look uneven. Also, relax as you stitch! If you pull the thread too hard it bunches up the fabric. The stitches should lie flat on the fabric.

6 Stitch from the middle outward to ensure that you don't stitch off the edge of the material. Count the number of squares in one area of the pattern and then stitch the same number, in the same arrangement, on the fabric.

Count the spaces in between stitches too, and keep checking that you are following the pattern correctly. It may help to enlarge and photocopy the pattern and cross through the squares when you have stitched them.

7 Whenever you finish with a length of thread, secure it on the back of the material by pulling the needle through the back of some stitches. Remember to use only two strands of the thread when you start stitching again.

8 Once finished, wash the final piece in a sink of cold water and a tiny amount of mild handwash detergent. Rinse it out very thoroughly and place it on a towel on the floor. Fold the towel over the cross-stitch and roll it up with the cross-stitch piece inside. Step on the rolled up towel a few times, to help draw the water out of the cross-stitch. Remove the towel and hang up the cross-stitch until it's dry. Never put it in the tumble drier!

9 Iron your design on a low heat—if the iron is too hot it will burn the thread. Be extra careful and put some thin cotton material between the cross-stitch and the iron.

10 At this point you can cut any excess fabric from around the design, but think about what want to do with it first. You can stick it straight up on the wall or frame it. You could hang it up like a flag on a pirate ship, or wear it on your shirt for an extra spooky Halloween!

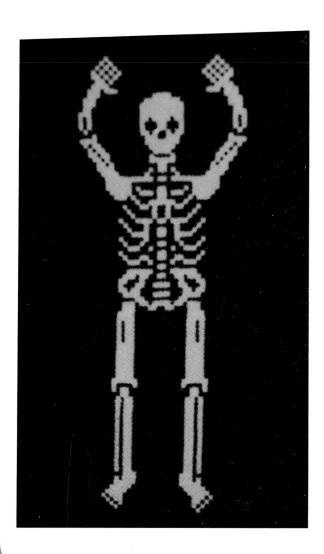

tip

If you are really having a hard time getting started, just look up "animated cross stitch" on an Internet search engine like Google. There are many sources on the web that can show you the process animated. Honestly, it's really very simple, especially once you see an example.

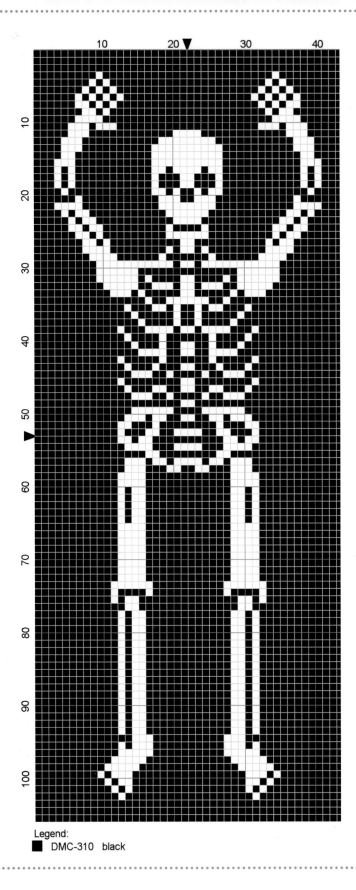

Legend:
■ DMC-310   black

42

BLEACH PARTY

CHLOE BURROW

Get the party started with a bottle of bleach and a punk rock design. Copy Chloe's perfectly off-kilter letters of different sizes and styles, or cut and paste your own message.

MATERIALS

- Clean cotton t-shirt in a strong colour
- Bottle of bleach
- Pair of rubber gloves
- Old stiff-bristle brush
- Sheet of clear acetate big enough to cover your design
- Permanent marker
- Sharp craft knife
- Cutting mat or an old piece of floor lino
- Metal ruler
- Spray mount
- Masking tape

INSTRUCTIONS

1 Photocopy the template on page 115. You can enlarge it to fit the size of your t-shirt.

2 Lay an acetate sheet over the design, using strips of masking tape to hold the design and the acetate in place. Trace the outlines of the letters with the permanent marker.

3 Place the acetate onto a cutting mat and attach with some masking tape. Carefully cut out your stencil using a sharp craft knife and metal ruler. Take care over letters with loops, such as 'a', 'b', 'e', 'o', 'p' etc.. If you lose part of the stencil, you can always stick bits back on with masking tape.

4 Due to the fumes that the bleach produces, you must do this next part outdoors, or at least by an open window. Place the t-shirt on a flat surface and put an old towel or several sheets of newspaper in between the front and the back to avoid bleaching the back as well!

5 Spray the back of the stencil lightly with spray mount. Wait 10 seconds for the spray to go tacky and then press the stencil onto the front of the t-shirt.

6 Bleach is a strong, highly toxic chemical and when using it you must wear rubber gloves to protect your skin and an apron (see page 13 for DIY ideas) to protect your clothes. Pour some bleach into a cup and use the brush to apply by using small amounts of bleach and moving the brush from the outside of the letter inwards, so as to avoid bleaching under the stencil.

7 Depending on the darkness of the colour of the t-shirt, the bleach may need several applications over a couple of hours before all the letters are fully bleached out.

8 When you are happy with the effect, allow the bleach to dry before removing the stencil. For added punk appeal, flick some bleach over the design.

9 Run the t-shirt under cold water and wash your t-shirt in the washing machine to remove any remaining bleach.

tips

You can also use stencils bought from a stationery shop—although these will only come in standard letter sizes and styles. Alternatively, download letters and symbols from the Internet (just type 'free stencils' into a search engine).

Create your own design by cutting out letters from newspaper headlines and arranging them on a piece of A4 (8.3×11.7 in) paper. When you are happy with design, stick the letters down and enlarge to a size that will fill the front of your t-shirt using a photocopying machine.

You can also use this stencil on a pale coloured t-shirt—just apply fabric paint with a sponge instead of using a brush and bleach, and follow the instructions to fix the design.

43

PINBOARD WIZARD

HEIDI KENNEY

This pin-board will make your room look really homely! It can house (ha-ha!) a collection of badges, or be used as a bulletin board.
For a really ambitious project make a number of houses and hang them side by side for a huge town pin board!

MATERIALS

- Two squares of cork approx. 25×25 cm and at least 1 cm thick—available at craft shops or at office and home décor stores. If you can only find thin cork, buy twice as much to double up the thickness.
- 2 pieces of contrasting cotton fabric 30×30 cm
- Piece of felt approx. 30×60 cm
- Craft knife
- Metal ruler
- Cutting mat or an old piece of floor lino
- Staple gun
- Scraps of fabric and felt
- Ballpoint pen
- Strong glue (look on the packet to see if it will glue cork or a similar material)
- Ribbon or string

INSTRUCTIONS

1 Cut one square into a triangle: measure along one edge and mark the mid-point with a pen (if the edge is 25 cm, mark the point 12.5 cm from the corner). Join this point to the two corners opposite with a straight line. With the cork on top of the cutting board, line up the ruler with one of the diagonal lines and cut with a craft knife. Don't try and cut through in one slice, as smaller passes of the blade will be less likely to make the cork crumble. Repeat for the other diagonal line.

2 On top of the cutting board, place the triangle on top of the square. You will probably need someone to hold the two pieces in place while you staple them together. with the staple gun. Staple all the way along the join. Turn the cork over and squirt a line of glue between where the two pieces meet. Staple along the join on this side. Leave glue to dry.

3 Whilst the glue is drying, cut the fabric into two squares at least 5 cm bigger than the cork square you are working with. Sew the two squares together by placing the right sides of the fabric together and lining up the edges. Sew a straight line (either on a machine or by hand with a running stitch—see page 32) 1 cm in from the edge.

4 Cut out rectangles of fabric for windows and a door, and pin them to the main fabric, at least 5 cm away from the edge. Sew around the doors and windows with a tight zigzag stitch on a machine, or hand appliqué with an overhand stitch (see pages 26 and 33).

5 Make a mouth with a running stitch and glue on felt circles for eyes.

6 Position the fabric face down on a table and place the cork house on top so that the fabric-join lies along the stapled line. Place a heavy book in the middle of the cork to hold in place. Take one fabric edge and pull it around the cork edge and staple to the cork. Work all the way around the edge, pulling the fabric as tight as possible. Again, it may be helpful to have an extra pair of hands, but don't worry about it being super neat because the back will be covered.

7 Cut away the extra fabric around the roof and cut a piece of felt slightly smaller then your cork house. Cut a small slit near the top of the felt and insert a loop of ribbon or string. Stitch the ends of the loop to the felt with lots of little stitches. Cover the back of your house with strong glue and press the felt down. Allow the glue to fully dry overnight and hang it on the wall!

44

WALL DECALS

SUSAN ROWE HARRISON

Shelf paper (also known as contact paper) is cheap and easy to remove (saving nasty disagreements with parents!). It's available in local hardware stores, but you can buy more interesting colours online.

• •

MATERIALS
- Roll of contact or shelf paper (the sticky one)
- Craft knife and extra blades
- Sharp scissors
- Cardboard or stiff paper
- Pencil
- Cutting mat or piece of old floor lino
- Rubber cement or painter's tape

• •

INSTRUCTIONS

1 Take some time to look at your room and decide what colour and pattern you would like your decals to be.

2 Photocopy the templates opposite, enlarging to desired size. Attach the photocopies to stiff paper or card using painter's tape or rubber cement. Alternatively you can draw your designs 'freehand' directly on paper or cardboard. If you would like to use text, arrange your text on the computer and print it out.

3 Using a craft knife, carefully cut through the photocopy and cardboard together to make a reusable stencil. It is sometimes easier to cut out the inside areas first by using a small pair of sharp scissors to cut around the outside of the shapes and finish with a craft knife.

4 Trace the shape lightly in pencil onto your contact paper to make a pattern to follow for cutting out the decal shapes. The stencils are handy to have in case you want to repeat several of the same decals to create a pattern on your wall. Don't forget the extra blades!

They dull quickly and "drag" through the vinyl contact paper and may tear it.

5 Following the lines that you have just made with your stencils, cut everything out. Don't worry if you cut through the decal—vinyl is forgiving and you can usually stick the tear together on the wall.

6 Once you have everything cut out, you are ready to stick! Don't worry if you do not like the placement of the decals. They are easy to move and readjust.

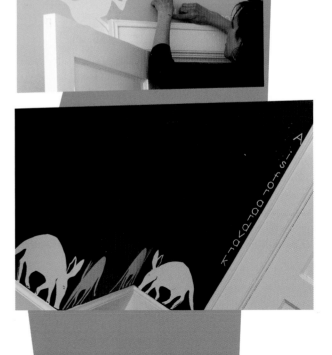

TEMPLATES

45

FORMULA WOODEN CAR

RACHEL MOGFORD

This wooden car is carpentry at its simplest. An off-cut of wood, two skewers and some wooden beads, and you're off! Perfect for budding young petrol heads...

MATERIALS

- Small piece of wood (approx. 10×6 cm, 1.5 cm thick)
- 4 big wooden beads
- Wooden skewers
- Wood glue
- Drill and drill bit (approx. 3.5 mm)
- Coping saw
- Sandpaper
- Pencil
- Poster paints
- Paintbrush

INSTRUCTIONS

1 Draw a simple car shape on the piece of wood. Use the template as a guide or make up your own shape. Cut it out carefully with the coping saw.

2 With a pencil, mark on one side of the car where you want the front and back wheels to go. This should be around 5 mm from the bottom edge, depending on the size of the beads.

3 Using a drill bit slightly larger than the size of the wooden skewer, carefully drill all the way through the wood at the marked points. Check that the wooden skewer moves quite freely through the hole. If the hole is too small, drill a slightly bigger one or rub the skewer with sandpaper until it slides more freely.

4 To measure the length the axle (skewer) needs to be, thread the skewer through one of the holes and put a bead on each side. Mark the length on the skewer.

5 Dismantle the car and cut two pieces of the skewer to this length. Sand any rough ends.

6 The car can be painted at this point; it's easier to paint before the wheels are glued on. Use the picture as a guide or make up your own designs.

7 Leave until the paint dries.

8 Finally, assemble the car by sticking the skewers through the holes in the car body. Place glue on the skewer ends before popping a bead on either side for wheels.

tip

If the holes in the beads are bigger than the skewer, wrap a thin strip of paper around each end of the skewer until you reach the required thickness. Apply a little glue to hold the paper in place.

TEMPLATES

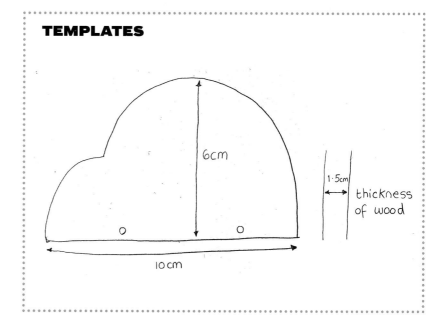

6cm

1·5cm thickness of wood

10 cm

① 10 6

② ✗ ✗

③ ✗ ✗

④ WHEEL
Skewer

⑤

⑥ Paint!

⑦ Dry.

⑧ Vvroom!

46

BLUSHING APPLE
POUCH

ANNA BUTLER

Get zippy and stitch up a fruity little change purse. Appliqué Anna Butler's blushing apple design for a look that's 'custom made'!

MATERIALS

- Undyed canvas, or other sturdy fabric, approx. 34×14 cm
- 15 cm zip to match fabric
- Blue, pink, white and black craft felt
- 15 cm of pink ribbon for zip puller
- Reel of silver, sparkly thread
- Reel of thread to match the canvas
- Fabric glue
- Sewing machine (optional)
- Iron
- Dressmaker's pins
- Ballpoint pen

INSTRUCTIONS

1 Trace the apple template onto paper and cut out. Use a pen to draw around the apple shape on the blue felt and cut out.

2 Cut out the separate parts of the template—eyes, cheeks and mouth—and draw around them on the correct colour felt. For the eyes cut around the white bits first, cut them out in felt, then cut around the black area.

3 Glue the eyes and mouth to the apple using fabric glue and glue or sew on the cheeks. To sew on the cheeks as seen here, use sparkly thread and an overhand stitch (see pages 26 and 33).

4 Cut the canvas into two pieces measuring 18×15 cm each for the back and front of the pouch. The length of the pouch is 18 cm and the height is 15 cm.

5 Pin the apple to the front canvas panel so that there is equal spacing between the top, bottom and sides. Again, sew in place using an overhand stitch in sparkly thread. Again, if you haven't mastered this stitch, glue on the apple instead.

6 Neaten the edge of the cut panels with the zig-zag stitch on your sewing machine or handstitch with a blanket stitch (see page 34).

7 On the front panel with the apple on it, fold over 1 cm of the top edge so that the rough edge is on the side without the appliqué. Press flat with an iron. Repeat with the back—although it won't matter which way you make the fold this time.

8 Lay the folded edge of the front panel on top of the left hand side of the zip—the fabric should be as close to the teeth of the zip as possible.

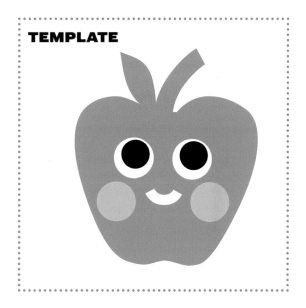

You will see that a 15 cm zip actually measures about 18 cm with extra tape beyond the teeth—so the zip should match up exactly with the 18 cm edge of the fabric. Pin into place and stitch a straight line across the length of the fabric 3–5 mm in from the folded edge, either by machine (use the zipper foot) or hand sew with a running stitch (see page 32) (fig. 1).

9 Repeat for the back panel on the other side of the zip.

10 Open the zip half way. Fold the fabric panels together with the right sides facing and the zip at the top, so that the apple is in the middle and you can't see it. Line up the edges and pin.

11 Sew around the remaining three edges of the panels to create the pouch, again either by machine or with a running stitch. Leave 1 cm seam allowance—this means that you sew 1 cm in from the edge. You will sew up to the teeth on the zip on either side (fig. 2).

12 Turn pouch in the right way around by pulling the bottom edge through open space in the zip.

13 Create a decorative zip pull by threading both ends of the ribbon through the hole in the zip puller to create a loop. Thread the ends through the loop and pull tight. Cut ends of ribbon at 45 degrees for the final touch!

tip

The Blushing Apple design could be added to a t-shirt or a jeans pocket.

fig. 1

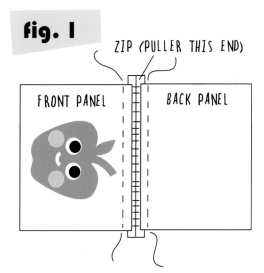

ZIP (PULLER THIS END)

FRONT PANEL   BACK PANEL

fig. 2

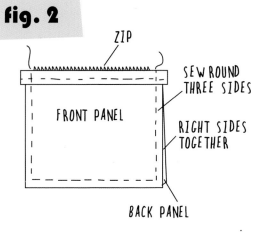

ZIP

SEW ROUND THREE SIDES

FRONT PANEL

RIGHT SIDES TOGETHER

BACK PANEL

47

FETE FELT BUNTING

NATALIE ABBOTT

Felted knit bits create a stylish string of bunting that will give a permanent party feel to your room—or balcony! This project can be either challenging or simple: you can learn a new skill and deck out your flags with a spot of needle felting, or just cut triangles and go!

MATERIALS

- Old wool jumpers
- Ribbon approx. 2.5 m long
- Needle and thread
- Optional for flag decoration: felting needle (in any size), foam block and merino fleece (get a needle felting starter kit and it will have everything you need, and instructions)
- Tailor's chalk
- Sharp scissors
- Bead/button (optional)

INSTRUCTIONS

1 Felt jumpers in the washing machine (see page 25) and leave them to dry fully before continuing. Once dry press flat with an iron.

2 Make the flag template from paper: draw a square 8×8 cm and on one side mark a point 4 cm in from the corner. Join the two corners opposite to this point with straight lines and cut out the triangle shape (see template).

3 Use your flag template and tailor's chalk to mark out about twenty triangles on the felted jumpers. Cut out the triangles with sharp scissors to ensure that the edges are straight and neat.

4 If you want to decorate some of the flags, do it now. Here are some ideas:

To make a flower, position the triangle on the block of foam and make a thin trail of mareno fleece for the stem. Felt the yarn onto the flag with a felting needle: you basically stick the needle through the fleece, the flag and the foam and out again. The barbs on the needle will mesh the fibres together. Repeat the action along the length of the stalk until it is firmly attached. Alternatively, position a piece of yarn and sew over it to secure. Sew on a button or flower bead.

For a teddy bear face, cut out a circle from the left-over felt and attach it to a flag with the felting needle in the same way as for the flower stem. Form the ears and mouth with merino fleece and felting needle. You could use fabric glue to attach the face and sew on bits of yarn for ears, etc..

5 Once fully decorated, attach flags to the strip of ribbon. Place the ribbon on a table with the patterned or shiny side facing down. Position the first flag so that the top of the flag is level with the top of the ribbon and pin (fig. 1). If the flag has a design on it, it should be facing up towards you. With a needle and thread, use a blanket stitch (see page 34) to sew together. Secure the thread and cut. Leave a space of about 4 cm and attach the next flag in the same way.

tips

Personalise the bunting with your name: cut out shapes in felt and attach with a felting needle, fabric glue or appliqué (see page 26).

Keen knitters can knit up their own swatches to felt into flags.

TEMPLATE

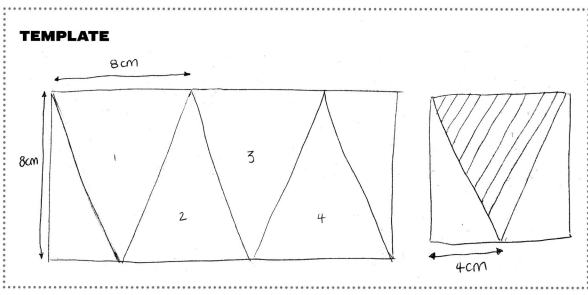

8cm

8cm

1

2

3

4

4cm

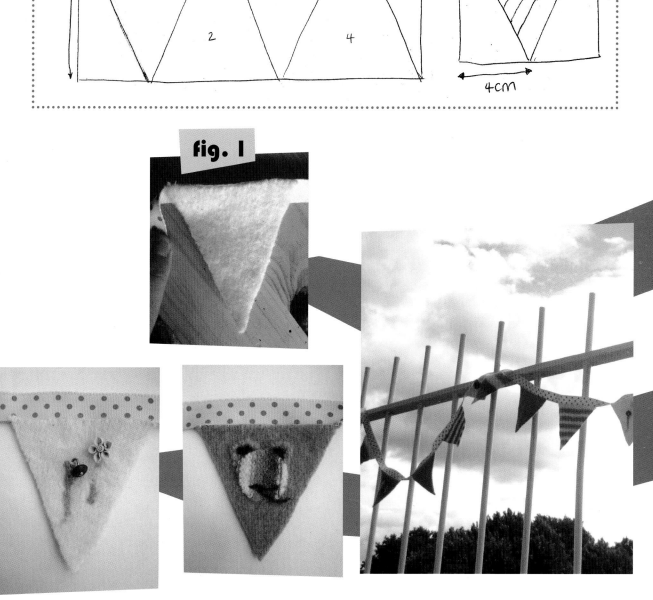

fig. 1

48

TOY TOWN

VICTORIA WOODCOCK

Rome may not have been built in a day, but in an afternoon you can whip up your own toy town. Hopefully you will know someone who has all the tools of the trade in their garage—then all you will need is a piece of wood, and some muscles to saw through it!

● ●

MATERIALS

- Handsaw for wood (better still, you may know someone who has a band saw...)
- Work bench and clamps
- Mitre box (optional but very useful!)
- Setsquare (optional)
- Ruler (optional)
- About 1 m length of square ended wood (don't use the rough looking wood as it will cover hands in splinters)
- Wood glue (optional)
- Pencil
- Sandpaper

● ●

INSTRUCTIONS

1 If you have one, clamp a mitre box to the workbench —this is a trough shaped tool that has space for the blade of the saw to go through, guiding the blade to a 90 or 45 degree angle.

2 To make a square(ish) wooden block, position the wood in the mitre box (fig. 1) and cut off a length of about 5 cm at a 90 degree angle (that's straight across!). Don't worry too much about exact measurements—houses come in all shapes and sizes after all. But if you don't have a mitre box, you will have to use a setsquare to draw a line across the wood at 90 degrees to the edge before clamping the wood to the workbench and carefully sawing along the line.

3 To make a modernist house: position the saw about 5 cm along the wood and cut at a 45 degree angle, with that the blade is moving towards the main piece of wood. (Again, use a setsquare to draw a 45 degree angle if you haven't got a mitre box).

4 To turn the modernist house into a traditional symmetrical house: turn the block around and from the same point 5 cm along on the other side, cut at a 45 degree angle in the other direction. To make sure you get this right, draw the line you want to saw in pencil first, even if you have a mitre box.

5 Cutting the modernist house into a traditional house will give you a spare triangle. You can glue this onto a flat block with wood glue to give it a roof.

6 Cut as many pieces as your arms will saw! To make a town hall or church, cut a first 45 degree angle as in step 3, but position the saw about 10 cm along the wood to make a taller building. Cut the roof into a point as in step 4. Stick a square wooden block to one side with wood glue. Place something heavy on top whilst the glue dries (fig. 2).

7 Sand all shapes thoroughly, rounding off the corners. Run your hands over the blocks to ensure they are smooth and splinter-free: then sand some more to be doubly sure!

tips

You could paint windows and doors on the blocks, but be sure to use non-toxic paint if they are for young children.

fig. 1

fig. 2

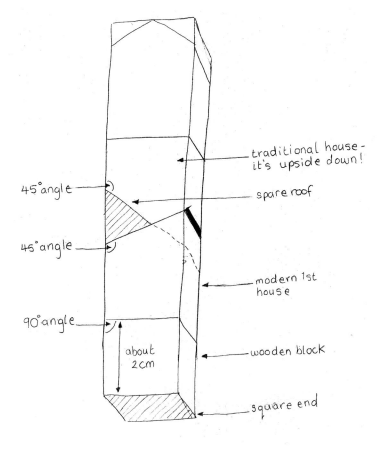

traditional house - it's upside down!

spare roof

45° angle

45° angle

modern 1st house

90° angle

about 2cm

wooden block

square end

TOUGH COOKIE

ADULTS ONLY!

49

TEA DANCING DRESS

SUSAN ROWE HARRISON

Who would guess that this cute dress is made from tea towels? Susan bought the tea towels in a local thrift shop for her kitchen, but chose instead to reinvent them as snazzy children's dress. Gem up on your sewing know-how before you attempt this project to get the best results from new, vintage or embroidered table linen.

· ·

MATERIALS

- Tea towels or napkins—enough to make 8 rectangles approx. 40 cm×13.5 cm
- Approx. 50 cm cotton fabric to match tea towels
- Approx. 80 cm thin ribbon to match
- Approx. 30 cm of 2.5 cm wide elastic
- Cotton thread to match
- 2 small buttons (optional)
- Needle
- Sewing machine
- Iron

· ·

INSTRUCTIONS

1 Wash all fabric before you cut, as some shrinkage may occur. If you are using vintage tea towels or napkins, try and remove any stains. Iron all fabric.

2 Take measurements around the chest (A) and the length from under the arms to where you would like the hem to fall (B).

3 The main skirt of the dress is made from panels of tea towels. Cut eight rectangles approx. 40 cm (or measurement B) ×13.5 cm (or roughly (measurement A×2 divided by 8) from the tea towels. On each rectangle, one 13.5 cm edge should be the hemmed edge of the tea towel, as this will make the hem of the dress.

4 Place two panels together, right sides together. Line up the hemmed edges exactly and pin. Sew a straight line 1 cm from the edge. Join another panel by placing it on top of one of the two joined-together panels and sewing in the same way. Continue until all eight panels are joined. Attach the first and eighth panel to create a skirt (fig. 1).

5 Finish by ironing the seams flat—run the tip of the iron along the stitches so that the fabric folds to either side (fig. 2). To neaten edges you can trim with pinking shears if you have them or run a zig-zag stitch along the edge.

6 The skirt will already be hemmed at one end from the tea towel edges. At the other end, you need to gather the fabric to pull into the chest. 1 cm from the rough edge, sew a straight line all the way around using either a long machine stitch or hand sewn running stitches (see page 32). If you are using a machine, do not secure the threads by backstitching, and leave long tails. Sew another line 1 cm below and, again, do not secure (fig. 3).

7 Put the skirt to one side to make the top bodice part and straps. If you are making the dress for a four year old (chest: 58 cm, waist: 53 cm, height: 102 cm) you can use the pattern provided by drawing it to scale on paper (see overleaf). Otherwise, you will have to make adjustments using the A measurement: Take the chest measurement A and divide by 3. Add the result of the calculation to the chest measurement, and then divide by 2. This is the length of the bodice piece and the elastic casing. Keep all other measurements the same.

8 Cut out the pattern pieces and place them onto the flat cotton fabric so that they are in line with the grain (so that the straight edges of the pattern run in the same direction as the edges of the fabric). Draw around the pattern pieces in tailor's chalk and cut out on the lines.

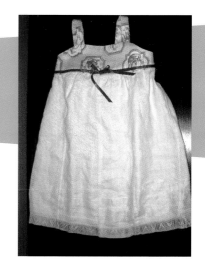

fig.1

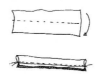

eight panels

fig.2

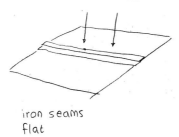

iron seams flat

fig.3

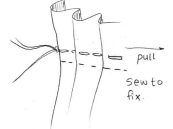

pull

sew to fix.

fig.4

fig.5

fig.6

fig.7

cut away

fig.8

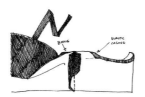

BONING   ELASTIC CASING

fig.9

BONING

SKIRT

fig.10

9 Fold the shoulder strap rectangle in half lengthwise, with right sides together. Along the long edge sew a straight line 1 cm in from the raw edges, leaving both ends open (fig. 4). Turn straps right side out and press flat.

10 Now pin the shoulder straps you have just finished to the bodice front (the right side of the fabric!). Trim edges of shoulder straps to follow the curve of the bodice. Sew a line through the straps and the bodice fabric as close to the edge as possible (fig. 5).

11 Place the second bodice piece on top of the one you just attached the straps to, right sides together so that the straps are trapped in the middle. Line up the raw edges exactly and pin. Sew along the upper curve 1 cm in from the edge (fig. 6). Along the curves cut out small triangles of fabric: cut close to the stitching, but not right up to it—this will help the bodice lay flat when you turn it the right way out (fig. 7). Turn right side out and press flat.

12 Open out the sewn-together bodice piece with the right side facing upwards. Place the back and elastic casing piece on top, right sides together. Line up the short edges at either end and pin. Sew at either side 1 cm from the edge (fig. 8). Turn right side out again. The bodice and the back will now be doubled and you will see the right side of the fabric on the outside and inside. Iron a fold into the back piece so that the rough edges are lined up.

13 Now return to the skirt and pull the threads to gather the top of the skirt so that it is the same size as the bodice. Tie the threads you used to gather the skirt and pin around so that the gathers are evenly spaced. Sew around the top to hold the gathers.

14 Now join the skirt and the bodice. The bodice has two layers and you want to trap the skirt between the two layers.

15 Match up the rough gathered edge of the skirt and the rough edge of the back part of the bodice so that the bodice part is inside the skirt (fig. 9). Sew through the skirt and the back layer of the bodice piece 1 cm from the rough edge all the way around. The front layer will fold down to conceal this join, so it does not have to be perfect.

16 Fold down the front of the bodice and press. You will see a rough edge on the front of the bodice. Fold under 1 cm of this rough edge all around and press (fig. 10). Pin into place and sew a neat line close to this folded edge, leaving a 3 cm space at either side seam in order to insert the elastic.

17 Insert the piece of elastic through one of the openings and pull it through the casing on the back. Use the second opening to help pin each end of elastic 1.5 cm beyond the side seams. Pull the elastic so that the fabric gathers slightly around it. Stitch along the side seams (where the bodice joins the elastic casing). You will be sewing through the elastic and all layers of fabric. Stitch the openings closed.

18 Pin ribbon 6 mm from the upper edge of the bodice, fastening in a bow at the front. Carefully sew a line in the middle of the ribbon.

19 Adjust shoulder straps on your model and pin to the back. If you know how to make buttonholes on your machine or by hand, you can make one on each strap and sew a button to the dress to attach. Otherwise, just tuck the strap into the dress and sew a line along the top of the elastic casing and at the seam of the casing and the skirt on top of each strap.

PATTERN

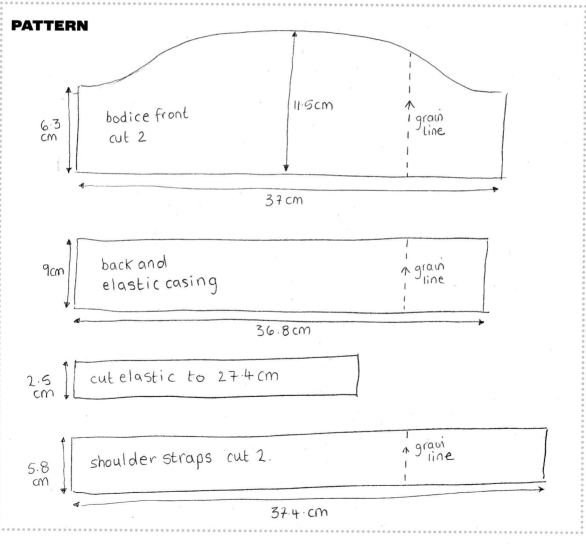

bodice front
cut 2

6.3 cm

11.5cm

grain line

37 cm

back and
elastic casing

9cm

grain line

36.8 cm

cut elastic to 27.4 cm

2.5 cm

shoulder straps cut 2.

5.8 cm

grain line

37.4 cm

50

RAG DOLL

AMY ADAMS

Everyone has clothes they no longer wear in their wardrobe. A rag doll is a traditional craft that is a great way of using up odd pieces of fabric, to create something really special to cuddle and treasure.

· ·

MATERIALS
- Fabric—patterned for the legs and plain for the body and face (pale pink, cream or brown works best)
- 2 large pieces of felt for the dress
- 1 small piece of contrasting felt for decoration
- 1 small piece of light pink felt for the doll's cheeks
- Polyester stuffing
- Coloured embroidery thread (for the facial features and the clothes)
- 30 m brown, black, red or yellow wool for the hair
- 40 cm ribbon
- 2 small buttons for eyes
- 4 large buttons for dress straps
- Needle and thread
- Dressmaker's pins
- 1 chopstick or knitting needle

· ·

INSTRUCTIONS

1 Enlarge and photocopy the templates opposite to the size required.

2 Cut the patterned fabric in half and pin the two pieces right side together. Pin the leg template on top and cut out two leg shapes 0.5 cm from the template edge for the seam allowance.

3 Do the same with the arm pieces on the plain fabric.

4 Sew around the arm and leg pieces, 0.5 cm from the edge, leaving a gap in the tops of the pieces. Turn them right side out, so that the seams are hidden. You can use a chopstick or a knitting needle to help with this.

5 Pin the body templates to the plain fabric, and cut out. You should have two pieces of body fabric.

6 Sew the body pieces together, by sewing around 0.5 cm from the edge and leaving a small 3 cm hole in the middle of the edge that forms the bottom of the body. Turn it right side out.

7 Fill all the body parts with stuffing, pushing it down with a chopstick or knitting needle to fill any gaps and smooth out the shapes. Be careful not to overstuff, as it will make the doll too rigid and could split the seams.

8 Turn in the open ends of the arms and legs and sew closed. Do the same with the hole in the body. Use a whipstitch as shown on page 33.

9 Stitch the completed arms and legs onto the body.

10 Using the template, cut two dress shapes out of one piece of felt. Using the contrasting felt, cut out two straps, one pocket, one underwear and six flowers.

11 Put the two dress shapes together, pin and sew the two longest side seams together, leaving the top, bib part of the dress open. Turn the dress right side round and put it on the doll.

12 Attach one end of the first strap to the front corner of the dress bib by sewing on one of the buttons with embroidery thread. Do the same with the other strap, then turn the doll over, cross the straps at the back and fix the other ends with the remaining buttons in the same way.

13 Fold the underwear shape in half and sew the two sides together. Turn it right side round, and save your doll's blushes, by putting them on under her dress!

14 Cut six circles of brightly coloured felt, and position them at even intervals along the hem of the dress. Pin another circle of felt on to the middle of them, and stitch them onto the dress using a blanket stitch (see page 34).

15 Cut out a pocket and sew it on to the centre-front of the dress using blanket stitch, leaving the top of the pocket open.

16 Cut the wool into 30 cm lengths, and split into three batches. Place the first batch flat over the top of the doll's head with approx. 4 cm hanging over the forehead for the fringe.

17 Attach the hair by sewing the wool down across the top of the head, using embroidery thread that matches the hair. Sew into the fabric and over a number of strands at a time.

18 Turn the doll over, and place the second batch of wool horizontally across the back of the head, beginning at the front and overlapping the seam of the fringe.

19 Place the third batch of wool underneath the second. Attach as before, but stitch down the middle of the head.

20 Trim the hair as necessary, and tie into two bunches with ribbon.

21 Now you have a completed doll, all you need to do is give her some features. Cut two circles of pink felt for the cheeks, and sew them on using pink embroidery thread.

22 Sew the small buttons on for eyes, and embroider features: eyelashes, freckles, and a few tiny stitches for the nose. The hair will hide any unsightly knots, so if you want to start from the back of the head, and work to the front, that might be easiest. Give her a name and a cuddle!

TEMPLATES

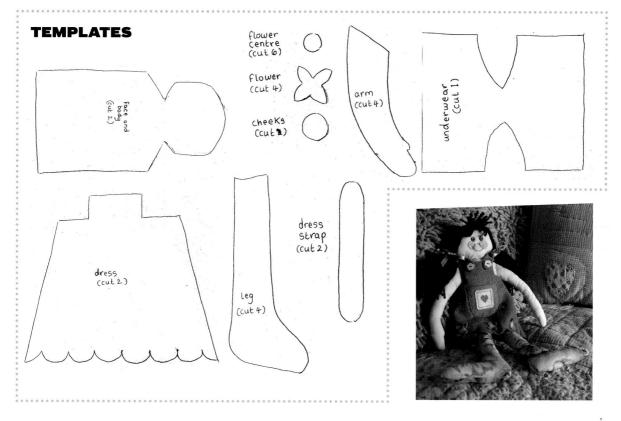

face and body
(cut 2)

flower centre
(cut 6)

flower
(cut 4)

cheeks
(cut 2)

arm
(cut 4)

underwear
(cut 1)

dress
(cut 2)

leg
(cut 4)

dress strap
(cut 2)

51

BASH IT TOGETHER BIRDBOX

CAMILLA STACEY

Bird nests come in all shapes and sizes, so see step 3 of Instructions to decide which bird you are building your box for. The birds won't care what it looks like, so bash it together for your feathery friends.

● ●

MATERIALS
- Piece of wood 15×150 cm and about 15 mm thick
- Wood glue
- Hammer
- Galvanised nails about 2–3 cm long
- Electric or hand drill and bit (use a 23, 25 or 32 mm bit if you have them, if not any size will do)
- Ruler
- Pencil
- Saw (if you can find someone with a band saw to cut the pieces that's easiest, or you can cut it yourself with a small hand saw)
- Workbench and clamps to hold the wood while you are sawing it
- Hinge and screws or scrap of leather
- Hook and eye catch for closing the lid
- Set of compasses
- Screw driver or bradawl

● ●

INSTRUCTIONS

1 Following the template, use a ruler to mark out the sections on the piece of wood. The inside needs to be at least 10 cm², but other than that, the dimensions aren't crucial (and if you are just making it for a monkey to live in you can make it any size you like!).

2 If you can get someone to cut the wood for you on a band saw it will make things a lot easier! Otherwise, clamp the wood to a workbench and saw along the lines using a hand saw such as a tenon saw.

3 Decide what type of birds you want to inhabit your box. Different birds need different size holes to get through—if you want to make a box for a blue tit then the hole needs to be 2.5 cm in diameter; for great tits it needs to be 2.8 cm; and for house sparrows it needs to be 3.2 cm. Clamp the front piece to the workbench and drill the hole in the centre. If you don't have a drill bit that big then you can use a smaller drill bit to drill smaller holes all the way around the diameter of the circle. Measure and draw out the circle first.

4 Using galvanised nails and wood glue assemble the parts of the bird box. You will find it easier if you have a workbench that you can clamp the wood to while you nail it. Start by nailing the side pieces to the back of the box. Add the front piece next, followed by the bottom piece.

5 You need to be able to lift up the roof in order to clean out the box each autumn. To do this you need to attach one side of a hinge to the roof and the other to the back of the box. If you are using a metal hinge from a hardware store it will come with small screws to place through the holes. Hold the hinge in place and use the screwdriver (or a bradawl if you have one) to dent the wood where the holes are before screwing in the screws. If you have a scrap of leather just glue one side to the roof and the other to the back—leave to dry fully before opening.

6 Attach a catch with one part above the hole and the other on the front of the roof. This is so that animals cannot open up the lid.

7 Hang the bird box somewhere that naughty cats can't get to as they will steal baby birds—the hole needs to be at least 13 cm from the floor. Hopefully next spring it will be a home to a fluffy family of birds!

TEMPLATE

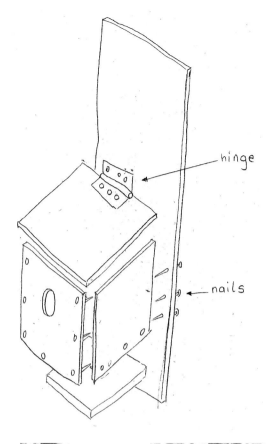

25cm — sides

20cm — hole

20cm — front

20cm — roof

17cm — bottom

— back

15cm

hinge

nails

APRON

LAURA FAIRBROTHER

A snazzy apron to protect clothes when baking, painting and generally waving mucky fingers around!

MATERIALS

• Hard wearing cotton fabric (patterned or plain)
• Approx. 160 cm strong cotton tape
• Matching colour cotton to fabric
• Approx. 1 m bias binding
• Pins
• Fabric marker or tailor's chalk
• Sewing machine
• Scissors
• Iron

INSTRUCTIONS

1 Enlarge the pattern by photocopying, or redraw to scale on newspaper. Cut out the pattern pieces.

2 Fold the cotton fabric in half lengthwise. Place the fold of the pattern pieces on the fold of the fabric and draw around them with the fabric marker. Cut around the pattern 3 cm from the lines (this is the seam allowance).

3 Unfold the fabric. Cut several small V shapes into the curved edges (fig. 1). Fold the curved edges over to the wrong side of the fabric and iron flat. Now learn how to use bias binding! Bias binding folds in half lengthwise to cover rough edges. Start at one end of the curved V-cut edge, and fold the binding half, catching the fabric edge in the middle to create a tidy edge (fig. 2). Iron and pin as you go. Carefully machine-sew a line in the middle of the folded binding.

4 For the straight edges, it's a bit easier! Basically, you need to hem them by double folding over the rough edge. So, start at the short edge at the top. Fold over the rough edge by about 1 cm and iron flat. Fold over the edge again by about 1 cm and iron. The rough edge has disappeared! Pin and machine sew two lines through the folded over fabric (fig. 3). Do the same with bottom and side seams.

5 Cut three lengths of cotton tape: two of 55 cm long and one of 50 cm long. Double turn under (fold over 2 cm and then fold over 2 cm again) the ends of the two longer lengths, and sew a strong square shape as shown in the picture (fig. 4). Fold under the end of each tape and pin to the back of the apron sides just below the curved edges. Machine sew with the same strong square shape.

6 In the same way, pin either end of the final length of cotton tape to either corner at the top of the apron. stitch the same shape to attach.

7 Double fold over the straight edge of the pocket and iron and sew as with the straight edges of the apron. Cut V shapes into the curved edge of the pocket as before and fold the curved edges over to the wrong side of the fabric and iron flat. Pin it to the apron in the desired position so that all the rough edges are hidden and sew around the curve close to the folded edge. Sew around again to add strength.

8 To add a utility belt to store pens and tools, cut a length of cotton tape 10 cm longer than the width of the apron. Turn under the ends and pin across the apron, with the ends attaching at the back. Sew vertical lines across the tape (fig. 5).

9 The apron can easily be embellished with an embroidered picture, appliquéd wording or a patch of contrasting fabric.

PATTERN

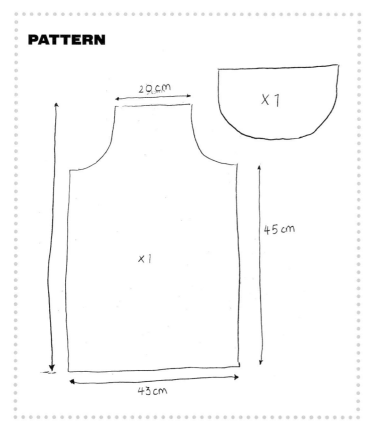

20 cm

X 1

45 cm

X 1

43 cm

fig. 1

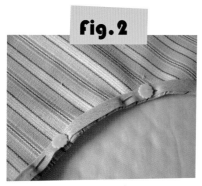

fig. 2

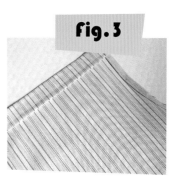

fig. 3

fig. 4

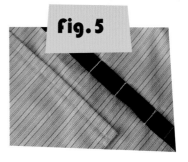

fig. 5

53

ON THE GO BABY CHANGE MAT

SUSAN ROWE HARRISON

Basic sewing skills are all you need to make your own colourful change mat that is easily transportable and can be thrown in the washing machine. Use soft cotton on one side and nylon that can be wiped clean on the other, for a luxury nappy change wherever you are. Add a pocket to stash nappies and a travel wipe box, and off you go!

MATERIALS
- Approx. 50 cm soft cotton—new or vintage (all fabric needs to be at least 70 cm wide)
- Approx. 50 cm waterproof nylon (you can test this by putting a drop of water on the fabric—if it rolls off, the fabric is waterproof)
- 1 m polyester or cotton wadding
- 2 buttons or Velcro for closure
- Old CD to draw the corner curve
- Tailor's chalk
- Dressmaker's pins
- Sewing machine
- Iron

INSTRUCTIONS

1 Cut a 70×40.5 cm rectangle of each fabric. Cut two rectangles of the same size from the wadding.

2 Place the two rectangles of wadding on top of each other and machine sew several straight horizontal lines through both layers. This is so that they will hold together in the wash.

3 Use tailor's chalk and the CD to draw a gentle curve at the corners of the layers of wadding and the fabric rectangles. Cut along the chalk lines. Place to one side.

4 To make a pocket, measure the width and height of the items you would like to carry, and cut two pieces of fabric (one in waterproof fabric, one in cotton) slightly larger than your measurements.

5 Pin the two pocket pieces together with right sides facing. Machine stitch around the rectangle 1 cm in from the edge, leaving an opening along what will be the bottom of the pocket (fig. 1).Turn the pocket right side out and iron flat, tucking in the raw edges of the opening so that all edges look neat and finished.

6 If you have decided to use buttons to fasten the mat, rather than Velcro, you need to make two loops from the fabric. To do so, cut a piece of fabric approx. 20×5 cm for each loop and fold lengthwise with the right sides together. Pin to hold the fold in place and sew a straight line 1 cm in from the cut edge. Turn right side out and iron flat. Sew a straight line along the middle of the fabric strip: this will add strength and keep the loops flat.

7 Now evenly space the loops into the opening in the pocket and pin into place, adjusting the length so that it will fasten around the button. Sew a couple of stitches to secure. If you are using Velcro, position two pieces with hooks along the edge with the opening and sew or stick into place.

8 Now return to the mat pieces and pin the pocket to the cotton piece towards one end in the centre. The top edge of the pocket without the loops or Velcro should be at least 4 cm from the fabric edge. Leave the side close to the edge open for the pocket opening and sew along the three other sides close to the edge (fig. 2). Sew along all three sides again for strength.

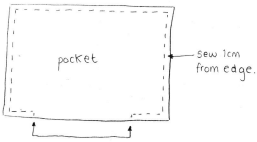

fig. 1

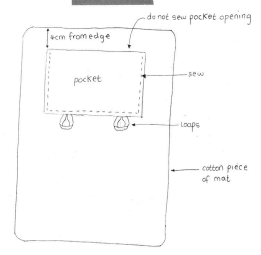

pocket

sew 1cm from edge.

gap to turn right side out and insert loops.

9 Place the two layers of fabric on top of each other with the right sides facing so the pocket will be in the middle. Place the wadding on top and pin all three layers together. Machine stitch around the mat 1 cm in from the edge, leaving an opening at least 10 cm wide to turn the mat right side out.

10 Turn mat right side out and iron flat, making sure that the seam is at the edge of the mat all the way around. Fold the fabric edges at the opening, iron and pin.

11 Carefully sew a line all the way around the mat 1 cm in from the edge.

12 Fold the mat into thirds with the cotton fabric on the outside, and the opposite end of the mat folding over the pocket. Position the buttons on the top of this flap, so that they line up with the loops. Sew on buttons and *voila*! (If you are using Velcro, the corresponding fluffy pieces need to go on the inside of the flap to connect with the hooked pieces).

fig. 2

do not sew pocket opening

4cm from edge

pocket

sew

loops

cotton piece of mat

54

BITS AND BOBS PATCHWORK BIB

MELISSA HAWORTH

Patchwork is a great way to use up odds and ends of fabric and unlike making a quilt, a bib is a quick and simple project. This pattern is generously sized so great for a toddler; just adjust it to make it a bit smaller for a new baby.

MATERIALS

- Long, thin scraps of 100 per cent cotton quilting fabric
- 1 piece of coordinating cotton fabric and 1 piece of plain flannel each 10×15 inches (25.4×38.1 cm)
- Snap and snap-setter or iron-on Velcro
- Thread
- Scissors
- Sewing machine
- Pins
- Ruler
- Ballpoint pen
- Dressmaker's pins
- Tailor's chalk

INSTRUCTIONS

1 Choose four to eight scraps of coordinating cotton fabrics and cut them into 8 cm wide strips of different lengths lengths up to 25 cm.

2 Sew the strips end to end by placing two pieces on top of one another, right sides together and sewing a straight line 0.5 cm from the short edge. Open right side out. Keep adding strips in the same way until the piece is at least 40 cm long. Make another three rows altering the positioning of the seams for a random look (see photo).

3 Sew the four rows side to side by placing the right sides of two pieces at a time together and sewing 0.5 cm from the long edge. Iron the completed patchwork piece.

4 Enlarge, photocopy and trace the bib pattern on the 25×40 cm flannel rectangle. Fold in half vertically so your bib is symmetrical and cut out the flannel pattern.

5 Lay the cotton fabric right side up and place the patchwork piece on top, right side down (so right sides together). Place the flannel template on top of the other two layers. Make sure the stripes of patchwork are perfectly vertical and pin the layers together. Cut through the patchwork and backing fabric around the flannel template.

6 Now it's time to sew. Starting on one of the straight sides, stitch around the bib 0.5 cm from the edge of the fabric. Be sure to stop about 8 cm from your starting point so as to leave an open gap where the bib will be turned right side out.

7 Carefully cut small V shapes into the seam allowance (the 0.5 cm between the edge of the fabric and the stitching) around the neck hole. Cut close to the stitch line, but not touching. Turn bib right side out through the opening.

8 Iron the bib so that the seam is at the edge and pin the hole closed with the rough ends tucked inside. Using a coordinating thread (this stitching will show) stitch around the bib 0.5 cm from the edge. Make sure the hole is sewn closed securely.

9 Follow the instructions for your snap setting kit and set a snap at the edges of the neck pieces. Alternatively, cut a small piece of iron-on Velcro and follow instructions for affixing it to the bib. Velcro makes the bib size more adjustable but the snaps make it hard for the toddler to rip off the bib mid-meal!

PATTERN

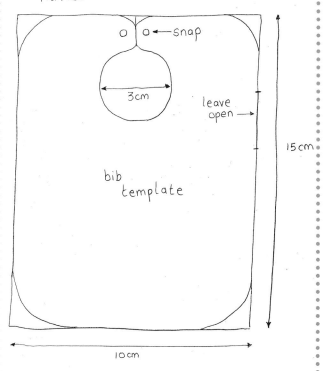

flannel

○ ○ ← snap

3cm

leave open →

15cm

bib template

10cm

tips

Make a two-layer bib with the flannel as the back with nothing inside.

Try a different patchwork pattern on the front or just use a beautiful fabric.

Add a pocket to catch crumbs.

Embroider appliqué on the bib.

55

MAGICAL FLOATING BOOKSHELF

LI JOHNSSON

A bookshelf—literallly! Wow your friends with this amazing book-as-a-shelf that seems to magically hover above the floor. Choose a book with a beautiful illustration on the cover or a funny title. Don't be shelf-ish—give it a go!

MATERIALS

- Screws that fit in the holes in the L-brackets— measure the thickness of the pages of the book (not including the cover)—the screws should be roughly the same length as this measurement
- 2 L-brackets (size L, at least 5×5 cm) per book shelf
- Screwdriver
- Drill (optional—but it will speed up the process)
- A large hardback book no larger than 15×25 cm and 2 cm thick (the book can't be read again so don't sacrifice a beloved first-edition!)
- Hammer
- Pen or pencil

INSTRUCTIONS

1 On the back of the book, mark two points 5 cm in from either corner along the edge that opens. Place the L-brackets on the marks, with a corner of the L against the edge of the book. With a pen or pencil, mark on the book where the holes for the screws are.

2 If you have a drill, use a bit slightly thinner than the screw to drill a hole through the back cover and the pages of the book at the points marked in step 1. Make sure not to make a hole in the front cover. Position the L-brackets and screw in the screws.

3 If you don't have a drill, get the strongest person you know to help you hammer the screw into the book. Position the L-brackets and turn the screw as far into the back cover as you can with your hand. Hammer in the screw a bit further. Once the screw is a little way in you may be able to use the screwdriver to turn the screw in the rest of the way.

4 Attach the L-bracket to the wall as you would a normal shelf (drilling holes in the wall, positioning rawl plugs and then screws through the L-bracket—get a DIY buff onto the case!). Stand back and marvel at the miraculous floating book! It is not strong enough to hold extremely heavy objects, but is perfect for a selection of your favourite books or toys.

56

MY RUCKSACK

CELINE REID

Get to grips with your sewing machine to stitch up these nifty little rucksacks that make transporting toys simple and stylish.

MATERIALS

- Approx. 50 cm of fabric—it should be fairly sturdy, (eg. canvas) for the rucksack to hold its shape
- 40 cm zip
- Iron and ironing board
- Sewing machine
- Sharp scissors
- Tailor's chalk or fabric marker
- Dressmaker's pins

For the appliqué personalisation
Flower
- 1 square of pink felt
- Small piece of ribbon

Car
- Contrasting small piece of fabric or felt
- 2 medium size buttons

Biscuit
- 1 A4 (8.3×11.7 in) sheet of t-shirt transfer paper
- Digital photo of your favourite biscuits
- Embroidery thread

INSTRUCTIONS

1 Enlarge by photocopying, or re-draw the pattern on page 147. Cut out the pattern pieces and draw around them on the wrong side of the fabric. Cut out the fabric on the lines (there is a 1 cm seam allowance included).

2 Start with the straps and the handle. Iron a 1 cm fold on each long length of the fabric. Then fold in half, lining up the folded edges. Sew a straight line along each long length close to the edge. Set to one side.

3 Iron a 1 cm fold on one length of each of the thin strips. Pin a strip either side of the zip, lining up the folded edges so that they touch the teeth of the zip. Use the zipper foot on the sewing machine to sew through the fabric and the zip close to the teeth.

4 Iron a 2 cm fold on each end of the strip—this will form the bottom of the rucksack. Join the bottom strip to the strip with the zip in it: pin the folded ends of the bottom strip over the zip by 2 cm on both sides to form a loop. Sew a straight line close to the folded edge.

5 The pocket: fold the top edge of the pocket down 1 cm, and by 1 cm again to hide the rough edge. Stitch this fold in place by sewing a straight line about 0.5 cm from the edge.

6 If you want to personalise your rucksack, now is the time!

Flower

- Using the template, cut two flowers and one half flower (fold the template in half for this) from the felt.
- Stitch the half flower to the top corner of the front of the rucksack by sewing around the shapes 3 mm from the edge.
- Thread the ribbon through the end of the zip and sandwich it between 2 layers of the flower felt. Stitch around the flower 3 mm from the edge, making sure to secure the ribbon.

Car

• Using the template, cut out the car shape in contrasting fabric or felt.
• Use a tight zig-zag stitch to sew around the car onto the body of the rucksack (or appliqué by hand—see page xx).
• Sew on button wheels.

Biscuit

• Take a photograph or download an image of yummy biscuits from the Internet.
• Print the biscuits onto the t-shirt transfer paper (if you use a biscuit with some kind of writing—bourbons for example—make sure to mirror the image in Photoshop first).
• Cut around the biscuit and transfer onto the front of the rucksack and/or the pocket following the instructions from the manufacturer.

7 Pin the pocket to the front of the rucksack, lining up the bottom corners.

8 Fold the top of the rucksack in half to find the middle point, and place a pin to mark. Mark a mid-point on the loop shape also by lining up the two joins at the end of the zip and marking the mid-point of the zip side.

9 Now pin one edge of the loop to the front of the rucksack: match up the marked mid-points on the front and the loop. Work around the edge pinning the right sides of the fabric together. Make sure you use plenty of pins around the curved bits. This will ensure a neat finish.

10 Run a straight stitch all the way around the loop 1 cm from the edge. Remove the pins, and run a zig-zag stitch along the rough edges to stop the fabric from fraying.

11 Fold the back fabric in half, and mark the middle with a pin as you did for the front. Pin your handle on the right side of the fabric, either side of this marker. The handle needs to be positioned so that it lies against the fabric. Pin the straps on either side of the handle in the same way, and at the bottom corners of the rucksack.

12 Now pin around the loop and the back as you did in step 9. Remember to match up the mid-points and open the zip at this stage or you will end up sewing it shut! When you have pinned around, make sure all the straps are inside the bag with only the rough ends visible.

13 Stitch around the same way as you did for the front. Go back and stitch over the points where the straps are again to make them stronger.

14 Turn the rucksack right way out—*et voilà*!

tip

You can use cotton webbing instead of sewing the straps yourself.

PATTERN

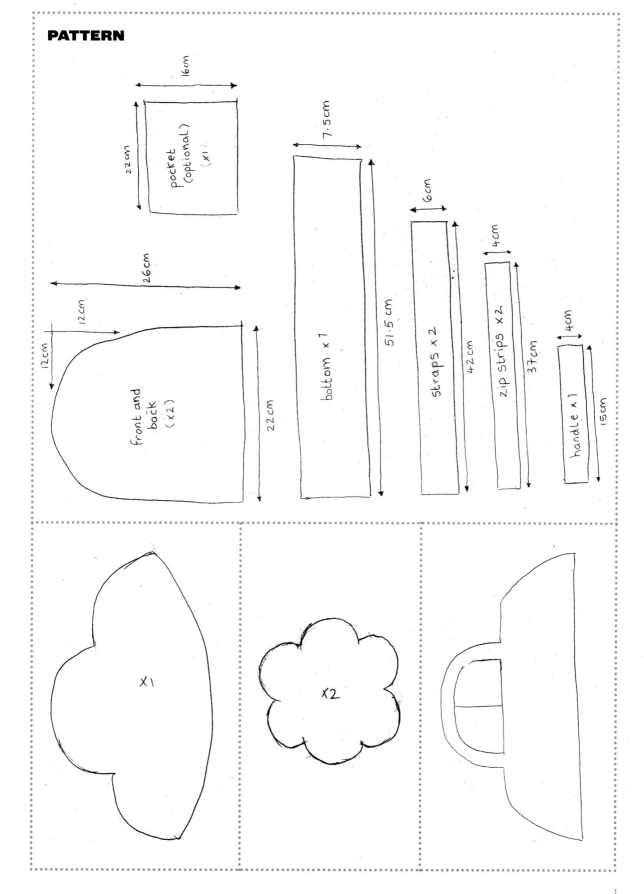

16cm

22cm

pocket
(optional)
(x1)

7.5cm

26cm

12cm

12cm

front and
back
(x2)

22cm

bottom x1

51.5 cm

6cm

straps x2

42 cm

4cm

zip strips x2

37cm

4cm

handle x1

15cm

X1

X2

57

CHEESY TOYBOX

WINNIE LAM

Do you have toys scattered all over your home? If your kids love cheese as much as Wallace & Gromit do, they will surely love this cheese toy chest. It might even motivate them to put away their toys on their own!

● ●

MATERIALS
- Clear plastic fillable ornament balls or baubles that open up to two halves, in various sizes: 5 large balls, 2 medium balls, 2 small balls.
- 1 cm thick plywood (dimensions shown in fig. 1)
- 2 hinges
- 4 castors
- Yellow paint
- Wood glue
- Wood screws
- Pencil
- Foam paint brushes
- Hot glue gun and glue sticks
- Corner clamp
- Jigsaw
- Screwdriver

● ●

INSTRUCTIONS

1 Go to a lumber store or hardware shop and get five pieces of wood cut in the dimensions as illustrated in fig. 1. 1 cm-thick plywood would work well for this project.

2 Use a jigsaw to trim the ends of side panels 1, 2 and 3 so that the ends are angled as in fig. 2a. The purpose is to angle the 3 side panels so they can form a triangle, as in fig. 2b.

3 Use a pencil to draw circles on the top panel and side panels 1, 2 and 3, by tracing the outline of the ornament balls. Fig. 3 shows approximately where to draw the circles on each panel, and the L, M and S symbols indicate the size of the ornament ball for that circle.

4 Using the jigsaw, cut out the circles which you drew in step 3. You will end up with circular holes in the top and side panels.

5 Using the jigsaw, cut out the loop part of the ornaments balls (fig. 4).

6 Paint all sides of each of the five wood panels, using the yellow paint and foam paint brushes.

7 Open each ornament ball and separate it into two halves. Paint both sides of each ornament ball with yellow paint.

8 Glue each half of ornament balls to the top panel and side panels 1, 2, 3. Do this by placing each panel on the floor, with the inner side facing up. (The inner side is the side that would be inside the toy chest.) Place each half of the ornament balls in the circular holes that you cut in step 4. Use a hot glue gun to glue the ornament ball halves to the wood panels.

9 Apply wood glue to the bottom edge of side panel 1. Place side panel 1 on the edge of the bottom panel as shown in fig. 2b. Use a corner clamp to clamp the side panel to the bottom panel. Remove corner clamp after the glue dries, which takes about one hour.

10 Repeat the above step for side panels 2 and 3.

11 Put a hinge near each of the two ends of side panel 3. Screw in these two hinges to side panel 3. Screw in the other half of the hinges to the top panel.

12 Flip the toy chest upside down so that the bottom panel is facing up and the top panel is touching the floor. Screw in four castors on the outer side of the bottom panel, with two castors along each of the long edges.

13 Flip the toy chest back so it's no longer upside down. Enjoy your cheese toy chest!

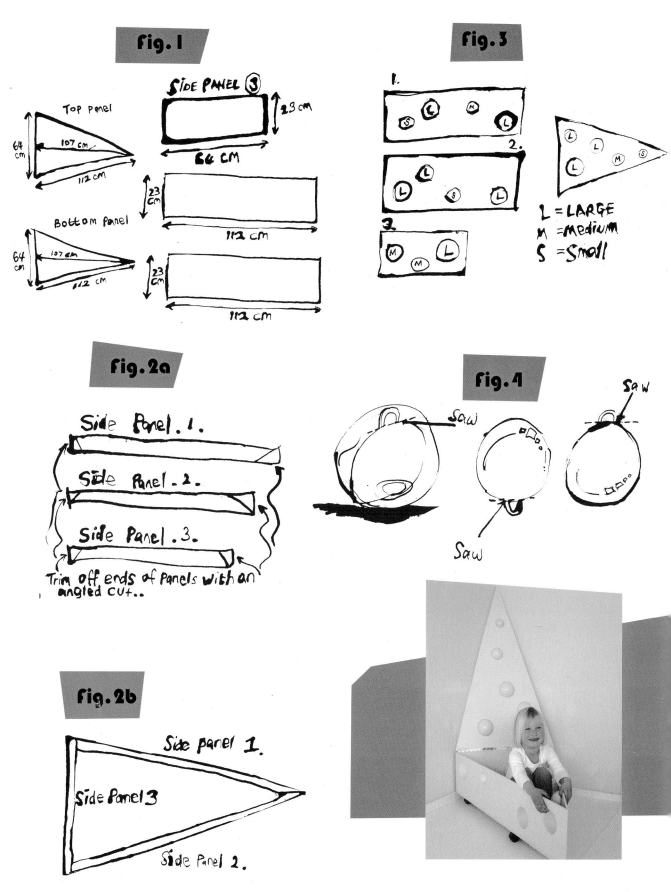

fig. 1

Top panel

64 cm · 107 cm · 112 cm

SIDE PANEL ③

23 cm · 66 CM

23 cm · 112 cm

Bottom panel

64 cm · 107 cm · 112 cm

23 cm · 112 cm

fig.3

1.

2.

3.

L = LARGE
M = medium
S = small

fig.2a

Side Panel. 1.

Side Panel. 2.

Side Panel. 3.

Trim off ends of Panels with an angled cut..

fig.4

Saw

Saw

Saw

fig.2b

Side panel 1.

Side Panel 3

Side Panel 2.

58

ROUND 'HUG ME' BEAR

LAURA FAIRBROTHER

A roly-poly cuddly toy for children big and small. Tweak and improvise to create a totally unique character.

· ·

MATERIALS

• Wool felt (two shades of brown are used here)
• Dark brown wool felt scraps
• Dark brown cotton thread
• Yellow cotton thread
• Black cotton thread
• Polyester stuffing
• Black embroidery thread
• Dressmaker's pins
• Fabric marker or tailor's chalk
• Sewing machine (optional)
• Scissors

· ·

INSTRUCTIONS

1 Copy, enlarge and cut out the template pieces.

2 Cut three panels from mid-brown wool felt and one from lighter brown. Cut 0.5 cm from the template edges for seam allowance. Cut four arm paws, four foot paws and two ears from mid-brown wool felt. Cut two ears from light brown wool felt. Cut one nose from dark brown wool felt.

3 With the right sides together, pin two panels together. Sew along the seam line on one side only (fig. 1). Repeat with the other two panels. Pin the open edges of each set of panels to each other and sew. Sew the final open side, leaving a gap to allow for stuffing.

4 Turn inside out. Stuff the ball, using small pieces of stuffing so that you don't get lumps, putting as much stuffing in as you can without stretching the material. Sew the opening up using a whipstitch (see page 33) so that it will be almost invisible.

5 Stitch (see pages 26+33) over the seams using dark brown cotton and an overhand stitch (fig. 2).

6 Sew the nose to the front of the ball using blanket stitch (see page 34). With black embroidery thread, embroider the mouth and eyes

7 Place the two paw pieces together and sew around the edges using blanket stitch (fig. 3). Leave the bottom open. Carefully stuff and sew up the opening. Repeat for the other paw and ears.

8 Use whipstitch to carefully attach each paw to the ball (fig. 4). Repeat for each ear.

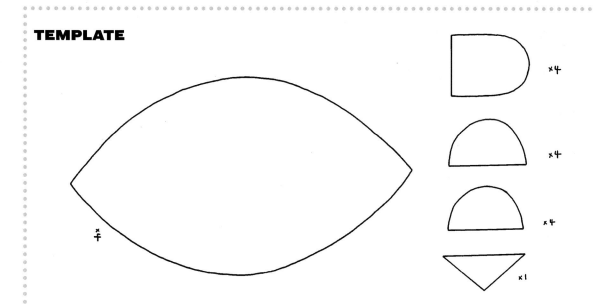

TEMPLATE

×4
×4
×4
×1

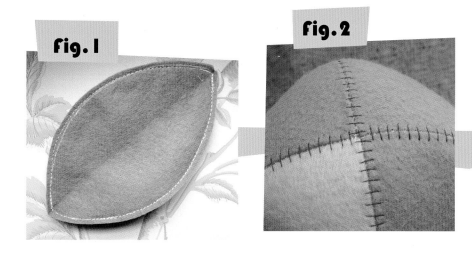

fig. 1

fig. 2

fig. 3

fig. 4

CONTRIBUTORS

NATALIE ABBOTT

Natalie is a textile designer whose quirky knitwear and textiles have recently been featured in *The Guardian* and *Elle* magazine. She has recently moved to West Sussex from London to concentrate on her Toxic Pixie range and can be found at www.toxicpixie.co.uk and at Greenwich market on weekends.

AMY ADAMS

Amy discovered stump work during her Art Foundation course, and was amazed by the technique. It gave her a continued passion for all things crafty ever since. After completing a degree in Weaving and Embroidery, she worked for a leading UK-based needlecraft manufacturer designing cross-stitch, tapestry, freestyle embroidery, paper crafts, appliqué, soft toys and dolls. Now that she works freelance she is re-discovering craft from a fresh, rejuvenating angle. http://lucykatecrafts.blogspot.com

ZOE BIBBY

Zoe is a self-confessed jack-of-all-trades. A freelance artist and maker she comes from a long line of arty folk whose motto/curse is: "Don't buy one, I'll make you one." After completing a degree in Ceramics, Zoe has spent the past 16 years teaching, shopping, travelling and parenting, but always making and creating. She lives in Wiltshire with her husband, two daughters, cats and a room full of junk waiting to be transformed into gorgeous items.

CHLOE BURROW

Chloe lives in London with her boyfriend, dreaming up elaborate DIY plans and saving up for a hypoallergenic cat. When she's not daubing t-shirts with bleach (which is actually not that often!) she studies Fashion at Central St Martins and is learning to built websites in order to launch an online fashion-centric DIY resource. She relaxes by knitting finger puppets whilst watching daytime TV.

ANNA BUTLER

After working as a fashion designer for six years, Anna decided to step out on her own and created Custom Made—a range of jewellery and accessories inspired by bright colours, pretty prints from far off places, quirky charms and recycled fabric and trimmings. Her handmade goods express her love of making things and she is passionate about keeping handcrafting alive, which is why she is working on a new set of Custom Made Crafty Kits to get people crafting at home.
Check them out at www.custommadeuk.com, info@custommadeuk.com. Custom Made has been featured in *N.E.E.T Magazine*, *Amour*, *Jellyfish* and various other publications.

TONI CHILD

A master cake-baker, poker ace, crack shot pebble-skimmer and general indulger of whims and fancies, Toni is also expert at making something from nothing. Her obsession with craft began at a young age, when she started hoarding household waste in order to create fantastical objects, like zoos from cardboard boxes and tiaras out of tinfoil! Now she's (pretending to be) a grown-up, she's started making things that are a little bit more advanced, like her fancy website for example (http://www.tonichild.com) in between doing research for a PhD all about craft.

AOIFE CLIFFORD

Aoife is a mother of two living in Melbourne Australia. She finds time to craft by ignoring housework. Living in the hope that chaos breeds creativity, she spends time cooking and making things with her kids. She is currently writing and illustrating a picture book as well as learning how to sew. You can follow her progress and other crafting whims at http://www.flickr.com/photos/33181946@N00/.

MICHELLE DUXBURY-TOWNSLEY

Michelle always loved to make stuff and be creative as a young girl, until sadly life seemed to get in the way! But then along came motherhood and now she is back doing what she loves and playing with lots of lovely fabric creating her own range of baby clothing and accessories. Michelle is totally passionate about doing her bit to fly the flag for the handmade revolution. She is responsible for launching prettycraftythings, a super duper alternative arts and crafts market, and Leeds Craft Mafia, the first UK member of the Craft Mafia family, on the unsuspecting folk of her fabulous home city.
www.yourasinineheart.com, www.prettycraftythings.co.uk, www.leedscraftmafia.com

LAURA FAIRBROTHER

After years of making puppets for animated shows on television, Laura got fed up of always making other peoples things and started to design her own. With a love of all things cute and a desire to create beautiful children's toys, Laura created her own handmade collection based around two fictional characters called Clara and Macy. This set of twins: one grumpy and bossy, the other quiet and sweet, set the tone for her toys. Working primarily with wool felt, linen, and cotton, Laura made her first soft toy in January 2007. She won an international 'softies award' a couple of months later, launched her label Cupcakes for Clara, and opened an online shop. Every toy is made with love, loveliness and care to create a cherished treasure just what every handmade craft should be.
www.cupcakesforclara.typepad.com, www.cupcakesforclara.etsy.com

SUZIE FRY

Suzie is a craftsperson working in Melbourne, Australia. The focus of her work has always been practical, durable pieces that bring a little handmade beauty to every day things. From clothing and jewellery to quilts and bags, Suzie's interests evolve as she explores new skills and materials. With the birth of her first child, Suzie became interested in toys and other objects for children. Her toys stand in stark contrast to the mass produced, throw away merchandise commonly aimed at children. They are centred on natural materials, particularly felts, and opportunities for imaginative and interactive play. She sells her creations and blogs about her craft ventures at www.soozs.blogspot.com

LAURA HARRIS

After graduating in Constructed Textiles at Middlesex University, Laura saw a gap in the market for her unique, handmade bags, and in 2004 she set up the label Laurafallulah. She began by creating individual designs for herself and friends, and now you can buy Laurafallulah in many shops around the UK. Her designs are inspired by her love of interesting fabrics, patterns and vintage design.
www.hannahzakari.co.uk, www.laurafallulah.com

MELISSA HAWORTH

Melissa doesn't have any crafting philosophy or artist statement but she loves making stuff. She started with sewing but is an equal opportunity crafter and happy to work with paper, glass, wood or stuff from the thrift store. When she's not crafting, Melissa can be found online at underconstructionblog.typepad.com or haworth.etsy.com. She lives in Sacramento, California with her husband and young daughter.

CINDY HOPPER

With a love of art, a keen eye for design and colour, as well as a Bachelor's degree in Art Education, Cindy Hopper is busy passing her creative skills on to her three children. Her family and friends are the beneficiaries of her passion for fun, creative projects, from testing new recipes for holiday treats to building floats for a neighbourhood parade. Find Cindy's un-ending supply of ideas for gifts, parties and rainy days on her blog, www.skiptomylou.wordpress.com.

JULIE JACKSON

Julie was not cut out for the rat race. Stuck in a stifling workplace with an idiot boss, she discovered the sassy side of traditional needlework and began selling cross-stitch kits online. Within a year, her kits were selling in national outlets such as Urban Outfitters and Target.com's Red Hot Shop. Her work has been seen in *The Washington Post*, *ReadyMade*, *BUST*, *The Face*, *The Guardian* and on *The Graham Norton Show*. She is a native of Dallas, Texas, where she lives with her charming husband and menagerie of pets.
www.subversivecrossstitch.com
Please note that Julie's website is intended for adults only, and some of the language on the site is not suitable for children.

LI JONSSON

Since graduating from Goldsmiths, Li has exhibited for Max Fraser's 'Design UK' exhibition at Liberty, 'ND Selection', DD '06 as well as '07, and the Super Design Market at London Design Week. Li thinks that it is just so much fun making stuff, so why wouldn't we? Grab the spanner and join the movement.
www.lovli.co.uk, li@lovli.co.uk

HEIDI KENNEY

Heidi Kenney lives in a happy brick house in a cosy little town on the edge of Pennsylvania. She likes to sew plush armies of cupcakes and toast. She lives with her husband, two sons, and silly dog Muffin.

When she is not perched at the sewing machine, she sometimes updates her blog and website at www.mypapercrane.com.

WINNIE LAM

Winnie is totally, completely, and thoroughly passionate about crafting. Her crafting specialty is home furnishings that are fun, whimsical, and goofy—just like her personality! She became devoted to making home furnishings when she purchased her first home a few years ago, and wanted to personalise it, and her design collection includes a cow table, mouth chair, chocolate sundae toppings and footstools. Her work has been featured on the MSN Lifestyle website, the Ikea Hacker website, and the BeJane.com home improvement website for women. So visit www.funnyfurnishings.com or email winnie@funnyfurnishings.com.

LOGLIKE

The London-based design duo behind Loglike take inspiration from inexpensive, biodegradeable materials such as corrugated cardboard, reclaimed wood and recycled fabric. They started producing their range of kids' and adults' hand-printed, organic t-shirts in 2007, focusing on simple, nature-based graphics. Quickly, they expanded to offer original gifts and quirky craft-kits, designed to encourage make-do-and-mend for today's world.
www.loglike.co.uk

RACHEL MOGFORD

Rachel has loved making things for as long as she can remember. As a child she would pester her mum in the supermarket to buy specific items because she needed the packaging for something she'd seen on Blue Peter. Her house is now cluttered with things she can't bring herself to throw away because they might be useful for making something! Rachel studied 3-D Design at university, specialising in wood and metal and she still loves learning new things. Rachel sells her crafts at local shops and does freelance work for a card company. When she is not making stuff, she is usually growing giant vegetables on her allotment or spending time with her little nephew Herbie who is keen to learn all her crafting skills. www.myspace.com/rachelmogford

CLAIRE MONTGOMERIE

Claire is a young, dynamic knitter with a wealth of experience in the craft and textile industries. She runs a successful online business selling her quirky knitted wares and teaches knitting classes at the trendy Loop Yarn Salon, in Islington, London. Claire also teaches textile jewellery courses at West Dean College in Sussex and children's textile courses at the artsdepot in Finchley, London. Armed with an MA in Constructed Textiles from the Royal College of Art, Claire is already building up a strong knitting and crochet bibliography and her latest work is *Easy Baby Knits* (Ryland, Peters and Small, April 2007).

JIM MORRIS

Jim is a freelance artworker and he helps all sorts of people to make all sorts of things. When he was young, he would make lots

of stuff with his sister and brothers helped by their Mum and Dad. Jim thinks that puppets are especially good fun because you can create your own unique characters. There's no end to the adventures you can have with them.
www.artgames.co.uk

NICO AND KATIE

Nico and Katie are best friends and like nothing more than meeting up for a crafternoon, a cake and a quick nip round the charity shops. They decided to name their craft business 'Ophelia Button' after a dream that Nico had about a very special little girl who could turn into a button whenever she wanted, and now everything they make uses buttons. Nico is the best at telling the buttons what to do and where to go because she has crafted ever since she can remember and buttons recognise her experienced voice. Katie does the knitting for 'Ophelia Button' which suits her just fine and fits in between her writing for www.tightjeansandjellyshoes. co.uk. Special creations and button treasures can be viewed and bought at opheliabutton.co.uk.

CELINE REID

Everything that Celine does is self-taught which shows that anyone can do it! She has always liked making things but got distracted by the corporate world. Thankfully, the arrival of Celine's kids put an end to that and reignated the flame of making things. It all started with a little bag she made for her daughter when she was very little. When Celine realised that there was no end to the possible combinations of fabrics and shape, she just had to keep making some more! When she sees something she really likes she often thinks about how she could make it rather than where she could buy it.
www.applejuicegifts.co.uk, http://applejuice.canalblog.com

SUSAN ROWE HARRISON

Susan is an artful crafter and a crafty artist in Toronto. She avoids the art versus craft debate and has exhibited her work in the North America, Asia, and Europe. For more information or to purchase her work visit www.lunule.com or www.lunule.blogspot.com.

ROSIE SHORT

Rosie lives and works on her narrow boat which is always moving around London. She started making dolls while studying illustration at Camberwell Art College and set up Bobby Dazzler with Jenny, Becky and Fumie straight after. Bobby Dazzler is a whole world of dolls in which each one is different. All are made from old materials and reclaimed buttons. You can find it at Upmarket on Brick Lane every Sunday and on www.mybobbydazzler.com You can contact Rosie at rosieshort@hotmail.com or via her website.

TRATINCICA SLAVICEK

Tratincica (Tinka) Slavicek is a London-based freelance puppeteer, working on creative projects in UK and abroad. Tinka takes her own puppets—Thingy Theatre—to venues and festivals, collaborating with other theatres to produce puppet creations, as well as making puppets and performing projects with children of all ages. Puppet-making is a way to make a sock with holes, an old teapot, a broken umbrella or who knows what else come to life and tell its story.

LAURA SPRING

Laura studied Graphic Design at The Glasgow School of Art where she spent three years successfully avoiding the Apple Mac by experimenting with her love of making things by hand, silkscreen printing and drawing. She now works as a freelance costume designer for a number of theatre and film companies in Scotland, alongside running workshops in costume and printing and setting up an environmentally friendly textile printing business with a friend from art school. Find Laura at www.mouseandbean.com.

CAMILLA STACEY

Camilla is an artist, curator and former playworker. She lives by the sea and spends her spare time at her allotment and scouring charity shops. As well as getting crafty in the garden, Camilla has made a name for herself making a line of vintage-inspired handmade goods called Made By Milla, (www.madebymilla.com). She couldn't have made the projects in this book without the help of her friends Max and Bliss, and the best nephew ever, Jacob. Buy crafty goods from Camilla at madebymilla.etsy.com, or read her musings at madebymilla.blogspot.com.

VICTORIA WOODCOCK

Victoria graduated a few years ago from Central St. Martins in Fine Art and now lives, works, knits and writes in London. For the past few months she has been moonlighting as an editor on *Making Stuff for Kids*. You can email her at www.makingstuff.co.uk.

WEB DIRECTORY

GENERAL CRAFT SITES

Enchanted Learning
An extensive alphabetised list of projects and activities, many of which come with templates and print outs. Great for schools.
www.enchantedlearning.com/crafts

Instructables
Tons and tons of step-by-step instructions to help you make all kinds of things.
www.instructables.com

How to Make Stuff
Constantly updated database with step- by step instructions on how to make a number of simple, to more ambitious toys.
www.howtomakestuff.com

Arvin Gupta Toys
'Toys from Trash' Guru Dr. Arvin D Gupta's shows you how to make loads of educational and fun toys at home. Full step-by-step instructions and photographs.
www.arvinguptatoys.com/toys.html

Whip Up
Billed as "A handcraft guide in a hectic world", Whip Up is an easy to navigate craft portal, choc-full of info.
www.whipup.net

Things To Make
Extensive catalogue of craft activities on a fun animated website.
www.thingstomake.com

Puppeteers UK
A gateway to the world of puppets.
www.puppeteersuk.com

Kids Craft Weekly
A great Australian site to help you think up ideas for craft projects. Sign up for the regular newsletter.
www.kidscraftweekly.com

Craftster
More ideas than is imaginable, craftster is an indispensible modern craft institution!
www.craftster.org

Softies Central
The fine art of soft toy-making—all the inspirations you'll need to get stitching your own weird and wonderful soft creations.
www.softiescentral.typepad.com

All Crafts
An organised directory of crafts ranging from sewing and woodwork to quilting and jewellery making. Free patterns and directions and many seasonal ideas.
www.allcrafts.net

Craft Bits
Many crafty categories for more ambitious projects such as soap and candle making. Also has instruction videos.
www.craftbits.com

Design Sponge
Cool homeware and lifestyle blog.
www.designsponge.blogspot.com

Handcrafters Village
Extensive resource for various handicraft techniques and design ideas.
www.handcraftersvillage.com

Crafty Pod
Tune your ipod to planet craft with this series of podcasts.
www.craftypod.com

Kiddley
Numerous contributors recommended Kiddley run by Melbourne-based Claire Robertson. Right now she's taking a break from craft blogging, but you can consult the archives, and hopefully there will be more on the way soon.
http://kiddley.com

Primrose
Julie Jackson rates Primrose's (aka Janet McCaffrey cross-stitch tutoral as the best she's ever seen. Check it out.
http://primrosedesign.blogspot.com/2006/11/stitch-school-cross-stitch.html

Purlbee
Beautiful website for sewing, quilting, knitting and other handicrafts. Lots of tutorials and patterns for stuffed toys and baby clothes.
www.purlbee.com

Susan Taylor Brown
Author Susan Taylor Brown's website offers tips of how to turn garbage into greatness and stimulate children's imagination.
www.susantaylorbrown.com/discards.html

Eco Artware
Archive of innovative eco-creations made
from recycled materials with instructions
and links.
www.eco-artware.com

Odd Collection
A unique auctioning site for designers and
craftsters to sell their one-off creations.
www.oddcollection.com

Crafty Crafty
Probably the best online resource for
alternative crafts. Hundreds of uploaded
project ideas- from building your own
paper city to how to crochet a skull. Great
photographs, instructions and links to other
cutting edge crafty media.
www.craftycrafty.tv

● ● ● ● ● ● ● ● ● ● ● ● ● ● ● ● ● ●

CHILDREN'S PARTIES

● ● ● ● ● ● ● ● ● ● ● ● ● ● ● ● ●

Coolest Kid Birthday Parties
Fantastic site for themed birthday parties
with ideas, instructions and free printouts
to make your own birthday supplies
and decorations.
www.coolest-kid-birthday-parties.com

Piñata Boy
Great site on how to make your own piñata!
Step by step instructions to mould
a number of characters from Hello Kitty
to Medusa.
www.pinataboy.com

Knowledge Hound
How to make your own home-made
costumes for both adults and kids!
Many have step by step instructions.
www.knowledgehound.com/topics/
costumes.htm

● ● ● ● ● ● ● ● ● ● ● ● ● ● ● ● ● ●

PATTERNS FOR DOLLS, ANIMALS AND OTHER TOYS

● ● ● ● ● ● ● ● ● ● ● ● ● ● ● ● ● ●

Cloth Doll Connection
Invaluable resource for making an
assortment of dolls, animals and plush toys.
Full step-by-step instructions, diagrams,
templates and hints.
www.clothdollconnection.com/
FreePatterns.html

People Play UK
1930s paper patterns to print out, and
colour in.
http://peopleplayuk.org.uk/activities/
toytheatre/ & http://peopleplayuk.org.
uk/activities/toycircus/

V&A Museum of Childhood
Interactive pages from the V&A Museum of
Childhood. Lots of activities and printable
paper patterns to make toys from the past.
www.vam.ac.uk/moc/kids/index.html

DIY Data
Fantastic woodworking site with
instructions to build your own playhouses,
rocking horses and cars.
www.diydata.com

Knit Owl
Helps you design and create your own soft
toys with inspiration from Japanese soft toys.
www.knitowl.blogspot.com

Ravens Blight
Print out and assemble your own cool
zombie and monster masks, coffins and
creepy catapults. Perfect for Halloween!
http://ravensblight.com/papertoys.html

● ● ● ● ● ● ● ● ● ● ● ● ● ● ● ● ● ●

SCIENCE TOYS & PROJECTS

● ● ● ● ● ● ● ● ● ● ● ● ● ● ● ● ● ●

Thinking Fountain
An idea resource for scientific projects
and creations.
www.thinkingfountain.org

Fun Paper Airplanes
Great site for flying enthusiasts! Fifteen
printable templates for the best paper
airplane designs, each with step-by-step
folding instructions and flying tips.
www.funpaperairplanes.com

Science Toy Maker
Nice little site for making a number of
scientific and folk toys. Full instructions
and diagrams.
www.sciencetoymaker.org

A Better Backyard
Useful resource for free playhouse and
playground building designs and projects.
www.abetterbackyard.net/
freeplayhouseplans.html

CRAFT MAGAZINES & BLOGS

••••••••••••••••••••••

Craftzine
Impressive US based online magazine available for both online and print subscription. Hundreds of craft ideas, how tos, recycling projects and children's activities. Also blogs and articles on alternative craft related goings on.
www.craftzine.com

Makezine
Sister site of Craftzine, promoting a Do-It-Yourself way of life.
www.makezine.com

Raspberry
Bags of bags!
www.raspberry.co.uk

Indie Quarter
Hip blog for independent designers, makers and crafters. Great photos, links to designers sites and information about upcoming crafty events.
www.indiequarter.com/blog/index.php

Craft
Extensive online craft forum and blog.
http://craft.co.uk

Makemag
Online 'Craft Community' where member share project ideas. Also free downloadable magazine.
www.makemag.co.uk

Belladia Typepad
US blog focusing on textile-based crafts.
http://belladia.typepad.com

Arts Crafts
Website dedicated to the history of the arts and crafts movement. Many links and articles.
www.arts-crafts.com

52 Projects
Modern website encouraging creative projects in everyday life. Great photographs, articles, blogs and links page.
www.52projects.com

Looby Lu
One mum's blog, featuring gorgeous illustrations.
www.loobylu.com

The Small Object
Beautiful-looking blog penned by a crafty mum Amy Karol in Portland.
www.thesmallobject.com

Ervilhas
Crafty Portuguese blog.
www.aervilhacorderosa.com

Wee Wonderfuls
This blogger's kids and the wonderful crafts that they inspire.
http://weewonderfuls.typepad.com

Paper And String
Follow the progress of this craftster's sewing projects.
www.paper-and-string.blogspot.com

Craft Log
Plenty of soft toy and sewing ideas to inspire.
www.craftlog.org/craftlog/archives/cat_toys_cat_and_kid.html

Little Cotton Rabbits
This mum blogs on her knitting habit and life with her autistic son.
www.littlecottonrabbits.typepad.co.uk

Molly Chicken
Sewing, crochet and soft toys.
www.mollychicken.blogs.com
Some material may not be suitable for young children.

•••••••••••••••••••••••

SUPPLIERS

•••••••••••••••••••••••

Crafts 4 Kids
UK online catalogue for arts and crafts supplies.
www.crafts4kids.co.uk

Knit Cafe
LA yarn/needle retailer and café.
www.knitcafe.com

Fun 2 Make
Great wholesale and retail crafters offering essential crafty supplies.
www.fun2make.co.uk

Fabrics Galore
Best fabric shop for choice and price
www.fabricsgalore.co.uk

eBay
For affordable haberdashery and all the fun
and fancy bits and pieces.
www.ebay.co.uk

Loop
Cosy and friendly London yarn store.
www.loop.gb.com/index.html

PM Woolcraft
British high-end yarn store.
www.pmwoolcraft.co.uk

The Paper Place
Toronto-based speciality paper retailer.
www.thepaperplace.ca

Wingham Woolwork
Largest UK-based textile and
yarn specialists.
www.winghamwoolwork.co.uk

Crafty Kids
Fantastic UK suppliers for unusual crafts.
Offers a variety of puppet and toy kits
and offers very reasonable interactive
children's parties.
www.craftykids.co.uk

Threshing Barn
Natural yarn and fabrics.
www.threshingbarn.com

Sew Essential
Super sewing suppliers to your door.
www.sewessential.co.uk

Click on Crafts
Glues, glitter, paper, pens, etc. All at the
click of a mouse.
www.clickoncrafts.co.uk

Texere
Every craft material your little heart desires.
www.texere.co.uk

ACKNOWLEDGEMENTS

This book would not have been possible without the generosity of the people who offered their thoughts, advice and time. All the contributors to this book took the time to write up their ideas, photograph them, and in some cases, illustrate them. For that, they have our sincere gratitude.

Thanks also to the people who we did not have space to include in this book for their enthusiasm for the project.

Thanks to Cindy Hopper, Aoife Clifford, Michelle Duxbury-Townsley, Heidi Kenney, Susan Rowe Harrison and Julia Woodcock for their help with the Introduction.

Thanks to Liz Cook for her instructions on how to felt, to Amy Adams for her instructions on how to cross-stitch, and to Kerri Sellens for her instructions on how to papier-mâché.

Thanks to Emma Gibson and Alex Daw for additional illustrations and to Raven Smith for additional photography.

Thanks also to Graham Black, Milly Black, Alex Sambridge and Nathaniel Hobbs.

Thanks to Zoe Louizos and the contributors for the Web Directory.

Special thanks to the staff and pupils of Newport School, Leyton for allowing us to photograph their crafting in action!

Edited by Victoria Woodcock with Ziggy Hanaor and Safiya Waley at Black Dog Publishing.

Photography courtesy of the contributors and Raven Smith.

Ideas by contributors as specified.

Designed by Emily Chicken with Rachel Pfleger and Julia Trudeau at Black Dog Publishing.

Black Dog Publishing Limited
Unit 4.4 Tea Building
56 Shoreditch High Street
London E1 6JJ
T   +44 (0)207 613 1922
F   +44 (0)207 613 1944
info@bdp.demon.co.uk
www.bdpworld.com

All opinions expressed within this publication are those of the authors and not necessarily of the publisher.

While every effort has been taken to ensure the accuracy of the information provided in this book, no liability can be accepted by the contributors or the publishers for any loss, damage or injury caused by errors in, or omissions from, the information given.

British Library Cataloguing-in-Publication Data.

A CIP record for this book is available from the British Library
ISBN 13: 978 1 906155 00 1

Black Dog Publishing is an environmentally responsible company. *Making Stuff For Kids* is printed on Garda Matt Art 170 gsm, an acid-free paper made with cellulose from certified forests, plantations and well managed forests.

architecture art design
fashion history photography
theory and things

black dog publishing

www.bdpworld.com

theguardian